HOW NOT TO BE A BESTSELLER

HOW NOT TO BE A BESTSELLER

A Collection By

Finn Mott

LETHE
PRESS

DEAR GENEROUS READER,

This will be unlike anything you have experienced before. This is a StandUp Comedy Set, a Poetry Collection, and a fabric of identity, culture, and transformation. Please try to have fun with its vulnerable and "taboo" themes. Note, the unconventional use of humor, satire, poetics, and "disboxed language".

Like any human, this is a living body. Inhale and exhale with its intensity and light.

This is long form, stream of consciousness, radical honesty. You will discover unique choices, diction, syntax that expand and challenge.

The first part is actual comedic bits I have performed on stage around the world. Keep in mind, while this can be "out there" and "raunchy" this all comes from a positive place with the intent to critique and progress the ways in which our society currently functions.

The second part is poetic fragments from around the world seeking the difference in how language works, and can be equipped to not only find ourselves and our voice, but also how we learn to overcome complex and adverse situations.

Everything is on purpose. The use of "body" is replaced with personal pronouns in some parts. Lowercase letters are used as a stylistic and societal device.

This is dedicated to those who saved me.

Part One

NOT A DEFENSE MECHANISM

act i

writing is an orgasm.
it is the gander of what it means to become
vibrance of creation lives at your fingertips
i thought i could make it to completion
without you
bare back
shoeless
sockless

i've made love to my writing many times.
        the amount of pure euphoria i find by placing myself—
        none other than abundant
the blank page is dependable,
        ready, sturdy, emotionally available
        it doesn't stir up unasked for emotions or leave you on
        read
        it sits there, and listens

in other words, writing is a climax.

> it can be physical or metaphorical
> it can also be the point at which everything else begins
> to fade

…
writing as vice

if i could imagine a world to live in, it would be sexy. a slow
> clap from any 80's movie or a sleepover with your best
> friend

there are roles we do not choose. voices we don't have

whatever it was reached for me

it let me know it was there before i knew i was alone

my love language /

wish to be famous

act ii

bisexuality was a harder diagnosis than cancer
because, let's be honest, male genitals are scarier than
        brain tumors
and what does that say about our society? the fear of battling
        cancer was less than the fear of being queer

when i was diagnosed with cancer, the doctors had a plan.
there were scans, treatments, a roadmap. but when i realized i
was bisexual? it was like stumbling into an escape room with
no clues—just a bunch of locked doors and unsolicited dick
pics from old men on grindr

when i was little i would dream i go separated
with no means of returning or finding them again
this is what learning to love is like

it took me two decades to realize that rewatching pitch
perfect over and over is not exactly the straightest thing to do.
i thought i just liked a cappella.

i feel as if an eternal riff off is taking place in my language,
trying to connect words across different rhythms

i saw an a cappella show the other night. nine 50-year-old
men in colorful pants and floral short-sleeve button-ups,
singing "if you wanna be my lover." and in that moment,
i thought: this. this is what america is all about. i was in
complete bliss. then my friend turned to me and asked what i
thought a beatboxer in bed would be like
and that was the moment i knew i would never know peace
or how to give head

how many of you got spanked as a kid?
are you kinky now? *me neither*

i finally have my sexuality figured out! i am attracted to
        lesbians and straight men
that's it. that's the announcement. please respect my privacy
        during this time
being bisexual is kind of like being hannah montana. you
        want to be a rockstar and a regular girl

did you know that a twink could be eating a twinkie, eating a
        twink, eating a twinkie?

i've come to terms with being nonbinary
most people don't really get what that means. so here's an
        analogy:
imagine cuddling. one person is supposed to be the big
        spoon, the other is the little spoon. but instead of
        a spoon, you feel like... a spork. a spork trying to
        eat soup. do i scoop? do i stab? do i just sit here in
        existential confusion

honestly, having sex as a nonbinary person is the same feeling
      you get when you successfully use both the spoon
      and fork part of a spork at the same time. it's rare. it's
      impressive. it's satisfying

the other day, i was talking to my mom about 9/11...
i asked her what she was doing when it happened
      she said, "oh, that was the day we made love, and you
      were conceived"
so now i have to live with the fact that my conception caused
      9/11
or security at airports

look, things have been getting rough
somebody called me a butch lesbian the other day... while
      trying to ask me out on a date. like the only time i ever
      get a girl to like me is when she thinks i am a girl
just to clarify—
bisexuality means two things:
1.   i am terrified of bugs
2.   i use way too many hand gestures when i talk

speaking of hand gestures—
having sex with a guy is like shaking hands. it's always way
      firmer than you expect. somebody's got to be dominant.
      and the motion? up and down. up and down. you get
      the idea

meanwhile, homophobic people treat genitals like badly
        trained pets
"sit. stay. heel. no, no—shake? no shake. get it fixed! send it
        to the pound"

on a more serious note—
i get such bad urinal anxiety that i literally just stand
        there and pretend to pee until the other guy leaves.
        sometimes i even make little water sounds just to sell it
drip. drip. drip
total commitment to the bit

when i give someone my number, i might as well just write:
"the guy you're gonna go on a date with, lead on, and then
        friendzone"

i am constantly amazed that men get women
i know guys who still use the snapchat username they made
        when they were 12
like, imagine trying to be sexy and saying
"hey baby, add me. @finnmcmissle15"

and speaking of past mistakes—
i just redownloaded snapchat, and my old bitmoji
clearly a version of me before i realized i was bisexual
white converse. jorts. a teal button-up with a flannel
the wardrobe equivalent of denial

you can actually tell someone's sexuality based on their
        favorite wii sports game:
tennis and bowling? bisexual
baseball and golf? straight
boxing? wild card

in bed, i need a girl who takes charge.
i need someone to just… play simon says with me
simon says: lay down
simon says: open wide
simon says: don't scream
simon says: call me daddy
i peaked in third grade
i had the bieber hair
i had my first sexual experience
she kissed me on the cheek behind the cubbies
best orgasm of my life

hypothyroidism gives me cold hands, which is deeply
        inconvenient when going down on someone.
like, hold on—let me just go warm up my hands real quick

girls say, "where are all the good guys"
babe, you just friend zoned them
(not speaking from personal experience)

my penis had an identity crisis and
i have officially started calling my penis "failure"
because the second it sees testosterone, it clutches its pearls
        and writes a mean poem about it

not that i really failed, per say but more or less felt like i did
nobody told me standing upright was nearly forgotten

why people have a problem with queer identities but love
charcuterie boards?
you'll mix crackers, cheddar cheese, prosciutto, and some
random jam
but two people of the same-sex is where you draw the line

i've also realized i have a terrible habit when i wave at people.
instead of a full-hand wave, i just… do this weird little finger
flick
like i'm lightly fingering the air

which brings me to my official list of songs that are terrible to
have sex to:
"i am moana" (existential crisis mid-thrust)
"this is me" – demi lovato (too affirming, kills the mood)
"the climb" – miley cyrus (accidentally too emotional)
"poker face" – lady gaga (already faking it)
"breaking free" – high school musical (accidentally too
inspiring)

i recently made a second gmail account.
which means i officially have more gmail accounts than sexual
partners

people are always surprised when they see me naked
like, "oh—hold on. let me just pull my penis out of my
        vagina
it's been screwing me my whole damn life"

and the other night, i had a hookup where the guy put
        eurovision on in the background.
we were supposed to be... engaging. but i was too distracted
        by will ferrell and rachel mcadams singing a terrible
        duet which i obsess
and that's when i knew
eurovision beats penis
and after we were done, the guy turned to me and asked
"are you a fem"
i said no
and he said, "well, you should be." honestly fair
at the expense of his own insecurity
as if nothing had happened
but i think the real problem was he was too short for me
then the realization i could be a top if i really wanted to be
so brave

act iii

my oncologist asked me how i was doing at our check-up.
i said, "the cancer made me gay"
the cancer keeps trying to get me to stick my own finger up
        my ass, but i'm too afraid to actually do it
i'm afraid that my finger might get lost forever, and i'll have
        nobody else to point to except myself

she asked about my sex life.
she asked, "have you had anal sex"
i said, "the cancer wants me to get hiv so it can have a partner
        in crime"
that when i lost my virginity, my girlfriend was on her period
        and didn't tell me, and i faint when i see blood—so
        that's why i like men too now

then she asked what i want to do with my life.
i told her, "i want to do something 'more' than being cured"
i want to be a poet, or a comedian, or a writer—or i can't
        really decide because the cancer wants me to be poor
        and die young

it's hard to dream when your body has given up on the future
but, hey, at least i'm living for the punchline

act iv

in a broad sense, the word "diagnosis" refers to, for all intents
and purposes of this book: confinement.
what have you been told that has willingly or unwillingly
defined you

this could be as large as a medical professional physically
diagnosing you with a chronic illness a psychiatrist
expressing a mental disorder you may possess some likeness
to, or as small and obscure as a friend telling you how you
look like the fictional character of flounder from the little
mermaid
what have you been diagnosed with

i
will
everything.
i will
person
you to
write anything:
for a
person with
chronic illness
laughter must develop
a new meaning
it
turns sick and twisted

it turns unlovable, and partly destructive
so we must learn to master this deep and dark art
we must learn to feel the capabilities of its core power
we must become ourselves within it, to arise on the other side

okay okay,
now that you made it this far
i can confess that i am not okay... but if you continue to
        believe such, i will not deny you
i will not use proper grammar or "good" words
i only say exactly how i feel. in all
the real reason i created this is because i needed to
while i was in the heart of my own darkness, the despair of...
        my... my own illness
i needed something precisely like this to help me overcome
        and move on

write your haiku
        here is an example
        we will start simple — 5 syllables
        with a regular haiku — 7 syllables
        it goes just like this — 5 syllables

out of nowhere this comet
crash-landed into existence
blew everything i knew
to smithereens
—a dinosaur when the world ended.
(getting blown up)

act v

you might be the only one who can
face the entire world
(little person with big tree)
you can consider me in part traceable through the footsteps
        of grief that look like a tourist attraction in any known
        place
this is my destiny, my secret to success as some might say
exploitation like fountains of water in a picturesque city
        center
you can consider my leaving a compliment to learning
a vow of silence to the noise you have made of me
a period to the unfinished manuscript

rearrange
the
parts of
you
since all of us here are one day going to be incredible and rich
        stand-up comedians
we might as well just get right into it and write your first joke
believe it or not, writing jokes is actually much harder than
        you think
it requires being extremely vulnerable and honest with
        yourself
in order to graduate from middle to high school
my 8th grade teacher assigned each of us with creating our
        very own bucket list

at the time, i thought there was little value in creating a list
        that is usually made by elderly people on their deathbed
        to say all the things they will never get to do
as i have gained maturity, i have realized there is something
        quite profound about writing a list of things you wish
        to do in your life
for not only are these things to check off, but they are even
        more—our dreams, our hope, our desires, our love
our bucket list is our life, in the most vulnerable post-mortal
        way
our bucket list is our diary of what we decided to do with our
        breath

act vi

i heard

mma playground
kids playing on a playground like an mma fight—
running, digging in gravel, pushing each other
one kid sitting on top of the play set, who will eventually be
        suicidal
you can tell who's cool

path i'm jerking off people say the path will come
i've been jerking off the path for a year now

the starving artist's dilemma
as a writer, i am professionally poor
and i will be dead before any of my work finds success
i studied business economics in college, which, believe it or
        not, is not actually that helpful in reaching your dreams
        as a starving artist
all it does is make you hyper-aware of how much money
        you're not making by writing poetry about trees

stereotypical cool kid
the publishing industry is kinda like that kid in elementary
        school—
the one who was always better at everything
drinking water without spilling it all over their crotch
running the mile faster than you

understanding fractions faster
and looked a little like you but was a tiny bit more
        attractive—
like, stereotypically attractive

existential dread
other than the publishing industry being filled with systems
        designed to screw over the writer and artist
        it's great
i really do love filling my life with existential dread
after i can't decide whether i should use a colon or semicolon

the struggles of being a writer
it's a good thing that being a writer isn't about getting
        published
rather, it's about having the liberty to make your delusions
        your only source of income

writer's block is like this
you're searching and searching for something you don't
        know anything about
and when you finally find that magical thing
you open your notebook
lift your pen up
adjust your grip
lean forward, dip the tip down just above the guiding lines
and when you try to push it a little farther to write
it stops you from freedom in that second
and you lose all doubt

sex and writing
kinda like when you're about to have sex—
you brace yourself for the rush, the uncertainty
wondering if maybe this wasn't the right decision
but hey, you're already here

awkward teen moments
i learned santa wasn't real the same year i learned porn was
        fake
that was a long senior year of high school

twenty one pilots is the reason i'm bi.
got a dumb dog to make myself feel better
girl bisexuals are so much cooler than guy bisexuals
angry birds gave me anger issues

my soft, white essence
put shower items on the edge
dog eats its own poo
i'm so white
i look off-white
i'm not vanilla, i'm vanilla bean. it's an acquired taste

gmail and old men
gmail is for gen xers
yahoo? myspacers
bisexual dog
taking things slow with a female
mouth abrasion

bargain store brands
bargain stores named after soft men:
ross, marshall, t.j. maxx

the writer's burden
i am a writer
not because i want to be, but because i need to be
i am a writer because i seek pleasure in getting screwed
        over—by friends, parents, lovers, the creative
        economic gig system that ruins the life of every
        starving artist

i survived cancer
because i needed to
or i found out i wasn't straight in a way i needed to
and, of course, both of those things are true
yep. true stories right there

trusting writers
not politicians
not tik tok news

writers don't lie
unlike these societies, writers don't lie to you
—the last time i saw my childhood best friend
i had just finished cancer treatment, four months late to my
        freshman year of high school
he offered me a vape

like, no thanks, i've done more drugs than you will ever even
           see in your life. have you heard of chemo
you should look into it. i think it could quit you
also, who offers cancer patients vapes

classmates with miracles and cum
sure, we were 13
our heads were filled with sperm, just pouring out the sides
except mine wasn't

the writer's loneliness
anyway, if you want to be a writer
you have to be okay with not having good close relationships
because i get all my material from those around me
jk

alien abduction, please
and, dude, it is hard being a writer
when i keep seeing ufo sighting videos on my feed
like, really? are we still on this shit
we know aliens exist—evidence enough is the way all of this
is
and if they do, why are we so surprised? so scared

abduct me already
at this point, i'm waiting anxiously
i'm begging to be abducted

lucky charms

did you know lucky charms don't have prizes in them
        anymore
did you know you can make meringue out of egg whites
weird shit is happening here and i don't want to be a part of
        it anymore

the disappointment

i have always felt this kind of disappointment in myself
even when i've done amazing things
like beat brain and spinal cancer
and then, predictably, do a ted talk about it
and write a book

not enough, but growing

i have always felt like not enough
partly because of what i lost to cancer
partly because of the "gifted and talented"
and partly because of my second-grade teacher who told me
        writing and reading were my two worst subjects

i am enough

but slowly, i am learning
that i am enough
and that just because you see someone else succeed or ask for
        help
it doesn't make you less

the politics of blowjobs
i guarantee if you take away every politician's mistresses
and just give them a guy who sucks them off
at least 50% of americans would stop believing the earth is flat

testosterone and the end of the world
of course, this would also mean the end of the world—
too many penises in positions of power, testosterone
exploding the planet

men and blowjobs
like most men, i am very good with my hands
like this—(typing)—if you like the full spread
or this—(typing on phone)—the on-the-go mobile version
takes half the time, same amount of pleasure

the great writers
the ones who write a poem that changes how we see
the painters who help us understand the human condition

the truth about writers
every writer i meet just tells me to run when nobody's
        looking
to get out while i can
to study something practical, like business economics
well, guess what? i studied business economics
and the only thing i learned is that 68% of the time
a straight man's favorite brand is patagonia or nike

bitcoin and cults
i also learned that bitcoin is just a cult
where old white men go to play webkinz together

writing and thrifting
writing is about trying to say what can never be said
writing is like thrifting
it gives you things you don't want or ask for
but need
used things
men and villanelles
like—if you are a man out there who thinks you're tough...
sure
but have you ever written a villanelle for fun

act vii

i'm bad at dating apps.
someone messages me, "hey," and suddenly i forget how to
        speak english

my dad texted me the other day.
just "hey!" like he was checking in from another dimension. i
        asked how he was. he said, "yes"

there's a way people turn pain into performance.
like, be yourself—but make it instagrammable

small town. one stage. everyone staring.

what's something you need to step away from?
the self-improvement section at target. or self disappointment
        section
pride merch in june is just temporary

bingo makes me question my entire existence.

breakdancing is in the olympics now, but race walking is still
        a thing?

at the vet.
they say dogs take after their owners. cool, so mine is
        confused about their sexuality

playing uno with family.
watching two dogs who should never, ever be allowed to
        breed figure it out anyway

ever see a guy lean back with his arm stretched out,
like he just unlocked the secrets of the universe

vacations don't start until you get food poisoning.
it's like your body's way of saying, "full system reset."
        nothing makes you rethink your life choices like
        sprinting to a bathroom in a country where you don't
        speak the language

people post about their morning coffee like it's their entire
        personality.
"starting my day right!" alright, put on a shirt

writers are endangered.
now it's all about platform, like we're just content-producing
        machines

i cross the street,
and suddenly i'm everyone's problem

it took me longer to realize i liked men
than it did to process having cancer

the scariest place i ever got lost?
a red-light district in belgium. had to ask a prostitute for
        directions. she gave me metaphors

what's one piece of advice i'd give myself?
airports are natural selection

feeling known is both comforting and terrifying at the same
       time.

once, i learned more about a person in a game of minecraft.
than i did in a year of knowing them

reading pop lyrics like spoken word poetry.

do business and make money,
or do poetry and die young

everyone in star wars is fruity.
chewbacca is a furry. darth vader is a theater kid with asthma

sometimes i think i could be a monk.

there's a kind of stalking that's really just keeping tabs on
       people you care about.

family is just a series of loopholes.

eating ice cream makes me question my whole existence.

i invited a straight girl to my comedy show.

i told cancer i wouldn't be its bitch.

i'm an ambivert.
i know because one of my balls is the life of the party, and the
    other is more of a quiet observer

when i see something naturally beautiful,
i make a sound that apparently resembles an orgasm

if i could give myself one note in life,
it'd be: don't rush the good stuff

backpacking through vietnam.
a lot of lost-in-translation moments. a woman asked if i
    wanted to "stick and broom." i don't know what she
    meant, but i'm not that into chores

someone told me i'd be more successful with women if i acted
    straighter.
joke's on them—i recently learned my love language is
    "feeling known" or coffee

anyway, vietnam was a spiritual journey.
you ever have food poisoning so bad that you start reflecting
    on your entire life? then you overcorrect, take too much
    anti-diarrhea medication, and suddenly, a normal,
    healthy shit feels like a personal triumph

cancer gave me a lot.
more than i ever wanted, but some things i'll always be
    grateful for

so here's my quiet little love letter to cancer:
you never loved me
you just wanted me to belong to you
but i don't
and i never will

chemotherapy: a love story
they say love changes you
so does chemo
one makes your hair fall out because of stress
the other makes your hair fall out because of poison

medical gaslighting 101
me: "i think something's wrong"
doctor: "you're young and healthy"
me: actively dying "oh, word? my bad"

cancer pickup lines
"are you a pet scan? because i feel like you really see me"
"are you a nurse? because i'd like to spend 12 hours with you
         but only get 30 seconds of your attention"
"are you chemo? because you make me weak, but i can't live
         without you"

how to get free applesauce
step 1: get cancer
step 2: tell the nurses you can't swallow anything solid
step 3: unlimited applesauce
step 4: question your life choices

the cancer glow-up
before cancer: "wow, your skin is amazing. what's your
        routine"
after cancer: "wow, your skin is amazing. what's your
        prognosis"
support groups & oversharing
support groups are weird. you'll go in expecting to talk about
        your feelings, and by the end someone's confessed to
        arson
and you'll be like, "damn, i just wanted to talk about my
        nausea"

inspirational cancer quotes that don't help
"what doesn't kill you makes you stronger"
bro, that's literally the problem
"everything happens for a reason"
yeah, the reason is cell mutation

a love poem for my tumor
you were never invited
you never paid rent
you just sat there, growing
like a man in his twenties with no life plan

cancer vs. my will to live
cancer said, "you're going to die"
i said, "bold of you to assume i'm not already dead inside"

chemotherapy: a love story
they say love changes you
so does chemo
one makes your hair fall out because of stress
the other makes your hair fall out because of poison

the art of the bald head
shaving my head was an act of empowerment
cancer taking my eyebrows was just petty

cancer's biggest scam
everyone's always like, "you're so strong"
bro, i'm literally just lying down

the make-a-wish dilemma
they told me i could wish for anything. a trip, a celebrity
        meet-and-greet, whatever i wanted.
i said, "can i wish for functional healthcare"
they said, "yeah... so disney or hawaii"

hair loss perks
no bad hair days
no overpriced haircuts
no need to manscape—just let radiation do the work

oncology office small talk
doctor: "how are you feeling"
me: "like i have cancer"
doctor: "haha"
me: "haha"
[uncomfortable silence]

32

the problem with cancer movies
they always show a sad, delicate person who looks hot while
    dying
meanwhile, i'm over here looking like a naked mole rat with a
    rage problem

medical bills are a horror genre
i survived cancer, but i may not survive this $80,000 hospital bill
the scariest thing i've ever seen is an "out-of-network" warning

radiation therapy: the sexy cancer treatment
radiation is just a glorified tanning bed where the tan goes
    straight to your organs
it's like getting microwaved, but your hot pocket is a tumor

the myth of cancer epiphanies
people assume getting cancer made me wise
no, it just made me bald and sarcastic

anxiety vs. cancer
cancer: "you might die"
anxiety: "but what if people are mad at you"
cancer: "literally, none of this will matter if you die"
anxiety: "okay, but what if they hate me"

hospitals are just haunted houses
•   flickering lights
•   strange noises at night
•   disembodied voices whispering, "code blue"
•   a bill so terrifying, you'll never sleep again

the cancer card
yes, i will be using the cancer card
yes, i will be skipping the line
yes, i will be winning every argument
no, i will not be taking questions at this time

"i'm fine" – the cancer edition
when i say, "i'm fine," what i really mean is:
"i'm existing"
"i'm a husk of a person"
"i'm holding it together... kind of "
but yeah, i'm fine

bald and beautiful
you ever have a stranger ask if you're bald because of cancer,
or if you're just going through a rebellious phase
like, yes, i'm channeling my inner 12-year-old—no hair, lots
         of awkwardness

hair regrowth struggles
they tell you hair grows back after chemo
yeah, sure. i'm basically a chia pet at this point
except instead of flowers, it's patches of sadness

chemo curls
after chemo, i started growing curls
it's not cute
i look like a 40-year-old lesbian trying to relive her high
         school softball days

cancer-related fashion
but i don't call it a wig
i call it my "temporary identity"
i went to dinner with my wig on, and someone complimented
me
i said, "thanks, it's cancer chic"

chemo side effects
chemo does things to you
it's like your body goes into a weird spa treatment... and by
spa, i mean a body horror film

the cancer timeline
people treat cancer like a big dramatic movie
but the truth is:
it's just like getting a coffee—slow, awkward, and full of
weird people staring at you

cancer is a full-time job
you think you're just going to get chemo and move on, but
no—
there are appointments, treatments, tests, insurance calls,
waiting rooms... it's like a job, except i don't get paid
for it
and let's not even talk about vacation days

exercising with cancer
they say exercise is good for you
so i tried a light jog
my body immediately went, "not today, satan"

post-cancer body
the good news: i can't remember the last time i needed a belt
the bad news: i also can't remember the last time i had the
        energy to hold my pants up

dating after cancer
the biggest turn-on
having your partner ask if you need help with your
        medication or a blanket
the biggest turn-off
having to explain to someone that no, i don't have hair
        growing in unusual places from the chemo

the fear of the checkup
the worst part of cancer recovery is the 6-month checkups
i mean, no one's telling you that the doctor is the gatekeeper
        to your life
it's like playing roulette every time they walk in with that
        clipboard

cancer recovery ain't pretty
cancer recovery is like the aftermath of a natural disaster
you can rebuild, but the cracks are still visible

the "how are you doing" question
people always ask how you're doing, and i've started giving
my honest answer
"honestly? still in shock i made it this far"

chemotherapy weight loss program
forget keto, forget paleo
the real weight loss program
chemotherapy
you'll lose all the weight. plus your hair, your energy, and
      your will to live

chemo is a loyalty test
when you go through cancer, you find out who your true
      friends are
like, when you're bald, throwing up, and trying not to cry, the
      real friends are the ones who don't ask you to go out for
      brunch

the two phases of cancer
phase 1: "i'm going to beat this thing"
phase 2: "please don't make me get out of bed today"

spirituality and cancer
everyone keeps saying cancer will bring me closer to god
but i think it just made me closer to the nearest bathroom

cancer survivor guilt
as a survivor, i often wonder, "why me? why was i chosen for
      this strange journey"
and then i remember, cancer didn't "choose" me—cancer just
      doesn't care

dating as a cancer survivor pt 2
if you've ever tried to date after chemo, you'll know it's not
      so much about chemistry—it's about sharing medical
      histories

life after cancer: the plot twist
you know you're a cancer survivor when you go in for a
      routine checkup and the doctor says "you're doing great"
but the plot twist is that you've never been more paranoid

act viii

grindr vs. hinge
making the transition from grindr to hinge is weird. one day
    it's, "here's my penis, when do you want to be bred?"
and the next it's, "hey! how's your day going"
i am not built for this kind of emotional whiplash

haiku about grindr
unsolicited
don't touch me, little rat man
oh no—i'm straight now

safe sex, safe friendships
my friend sent me a gift the other day—a 24-pack of deluxe
    condoms. with a note that said: "don't get hiv"
because nothing says i care like a well-placed all-caps psa
naturally, i sent something back. a giant, rainbow dildo with a
    note that said no promises
because friendship is about reciprocity

the fear of white substances
i have a lifelong fear of creamy white substances. ranch,
    mayo, blue cheese—i don't trust any of them. and i'm
    convinced it got worse after my first time with a man
a generic cologne of bark and cinnamon
a general anxiety, shame, sense of violation
my ending

also has a fear of creamy white substances. can't imagine
        where i got it from
like, i'm still not convinced that semen isn't just construction
        adhesive. you ever see what they use to hold bricks
        together? it's literally called caulk. no wonder
        construction is a straight male-dominated industry

male power
most people think male power comes from the penis. i
        disagree. i think it comes from the asshole.
hear me out—have you ever seen a man take a shit gently?
        ever walked into an airport men's restroom? it's not the
        sound of a civilized species.
a guide to being bisexual
step 1: don't

"a love poem"
it's not just a phase
it is so much more than that—
it is anal penetration
it is women making me their gay best friend instead of
        their lover
it is my voice, cracking halfway into puberty and then just
        giving up
it is not just a phase
it is me, all two inches of myself
confidently. mischievously
it is not just a phase
and no, i don't have hiv

and whether i'm a top or a bottom
we'll see
it is not just a phase
and it really blows—literally
because men are terrifying
but their pectorals? stunning
and i like to pump me up
it is not just a phase
i am me. and i love me

the autocorrect rage
it's ironic that i'm so good with words in poetry, because i
        am a terrible texter. autocorrect makes it worse
like, when i type "omw," i mean omw. but my phone insists
        on correcting it to "on my way!"
bro. sometimes i am just omw. not on my way

running from the man
i've been thinking a lot about my early life. even as sperm,
        i was running from the man.
and the man upstairs? he remarried someone 30 years
        younger than him. she's closer in age to me than
        to him.
if i can come to terms with having a sister as a stepmom,
        you'd think he could come to terms with me being
        bisexual. but nope
my life has turned into a bad porn plot—without any of
        the good parts

issues & dilfs

my issues have given me a thing for dilfs. it's funny how a
    lack of a before will make you irrationally attracted to
    men with good credit
so, if you're single… hit me up
i am an empath who loves someone who will hurt me

true manliness

i honestly think being "manly" isn't nearly as manly as being
    a woman. women literally create life
meanwhile; men start wars because they got called "buddy"
    at a gas station

halloween costumes

for halloween, i wanted to dress as the man upstairs, but i
    couldn't find a good ghost costume
i also thought about dressing as a straight person—just to see
    what it feels like to be loved.
what do you dress up as

tampon duty

in 6th grade, i was forced to carry around a pack of tampons,
    just in case a girl needed one
i never understood the logic. like, was i supposed to just
    sense when it was time? "hey, you look like you need a
    tampon. no offense"

horoscopes & self-improvement

i started reading horoscopes to become a better person. huge
    mystery why that didn't work out.

dads & emotional intelligence
i do not understand men. i have never met a dad who uses the
        same remote for the tv and the sound system
like, they'll program an entire home theater setup—but ask
        them to process an emotion? absolutely not

the grindr friendship complex
trying to emotionally connect with someone on grindr.
        you can ask him what he's into, but the conversation
        will always return to his small penis complex

ocd
i was recently diagnosed with ocd. there are two parts—
        obsessions and compulsions. and a third part: a disorder
my obsession? thinking i'm not good enough. when i told
        him i had ocd, he said, "good. it'll make you better"
        ah, yes. that's exactly how mental health works
most people have an inner voice telling them they're not
        good enough. mine just sounds like my ending…

act ix

i heard that funny guys attract girls

so

i consider myself to be an activist for the environment. for example, i have been thrifting because it is stopping climate change. i also spent $20 on a metal straw that i will use soon. i recently discovered that the word vintage is just another word for use. i have a big problem with this because it is not like i can just say that i am vintage even though my ex used me to fuck my best friend

this summer
a little boy who lived across the street from me told me that i talk weird. without thinking i told this 7-year-old that i will make him talk funny if he comes near me again. their family moved out later that summer

i have an iphone 8
and the other day a friend told me they miss the home button missing an iphone home button is like going back to a toxic ex because it was comfortable or missing the ex that would always make you do missionary because there was less room for confusion

act x

i've wasted too much time worrying about what other people
        think of me.
i've pushed away the idea that others are defining me by my
        disease. so, i came to define it for myself
i've held it under my tongue since the day it occurred

from here on, i will be a rich spirit,
not subject to its testament
in a life enveloped by its personal demise

i don't understand why every girl runs away
when i tell them i had two brain tumors
i mean, i don't even mention the spinal fluid, and by the time
        i do
i've already been friend-zoned as the gay best friend for life

i mean, it's not like i run away every time you get a cold.
was in copenhagen, right?
then, bam, a big guy with a well-groomed mustache and
        beard pummeled me in the ass

now, since i'm stuck convincing myself i'm straight
because of that first awful experience with a man
i'll never find a woman to love
because i'm a sensitive, soft-masc who looks like flounder
        from the little mermaid

no, i get it, don't worry. let the kid who had cancer
not get at least, like, post-sex awards
but nooo, you know what i got
seriously, do you want to know what i got

miracle sperm.
yeah, you heard me. i have sperm that's medically impossible
         to exist
my little guys came back from the dead
i have ghost sperm. phantom shit

and you know how a guy thinks with his dick,
well, i have a unicorn dick to speak to, and if i'm honest
all you big swinging ballers don't get shit where it counts

my sperm fucking sparkles.

and when my sperm gets its chance to prove itself,
it will fucking sparkle

but we have to get through this terrible rift in our country's
         political polarization,
because it's really getting me angry at the half of you who
         think sabrina carpenter is better than olivia rodrigo

act xiii

a precautionary note (ON SEX)

because you made it this far

i am impressed

really

i don't want you thinking i never had any fun

the most important parts of us often learn to live crossed out

the world makes us so proficient at lying to ourselves

that we forget what truth-making really means

when i was in the second grade, my school gave every
        student a dictionary

one morning, a peer showed me two pages

one for the word gay, another for sex

it seemed the people in charge of making the dictionary
        completely childproof

missed two small things—

and together, those two small things made gay sex

as if some godly foreshadowing

the torn spine of disorientation and bespoke curiosity

nervous laughter and hushed tones

the pages smelled of lust and language

the arrival of the search

at the same time, i was also being asked what i wanted to be
       when i grew up

my answer typically reflected husband or i want to have
       a family

now, of course, it would probably be best

if i married some sort of finance guy or girl

considering my very expensive and aggressively
       non-capitalist hobbies

it has always been difficult for me to separate love from
       friendship

my first crush on a girl was because she played soccer

my second was a girl i dated for two days in third grade

before she moved on to her next royal subject

in sixth grade, a girl pursued me

after a dramatic after-school encounter where i asked her out

she started calling me cutie over text

it was moving too quickly

at the next opportunity, i broke it off

in seventh grade, i had a long-standing crush on a girl

who i think is now a supermodel

we passed notes.

we spoke once

around this time, i also had a best friend i deeply loved

romantic or platonic—it was a matter of imagination

until i was diagnosed

and our relationship splintered irreversibly

by sophomore year of high school

i was still missing most of my classes due to illness

except one

taking a piece of text and rearranging it

to form another narrative, altering it visually as well

trouble is rising

hopeless raining insists

interesting, crowded

school teacher is—

breakdown

but art wasn't the only reason the class drew me in

i had a crush

her name was _____

to an extent, this was my first real like since cancer

i had little confidence

even less idea what i was doing

after months of drawn-out conversation

i built up the courage to ask her to homecoming

she graciously said yes

by junior year, i was finally healthy enough to attend school
    regularly

one day, a friend hugged me out of nowhere

i knew it meant something

we started spending time together

i gave her rides to school

eventually, i asked, what are we

she laughed. well, you have to ask me on a date

so i did

and she said yes

we went to a creek that ran through town

laid on a blanket

when we sat up, she grabbed my face and kissed me

a week later, she took me to a restaurant

she asked me to hold something for her

i held out my hand

she placed her heart in it

i have fell in love many times since then

but never quite like that

here is an incomplete list of people

who have helped me understand what i need in a relationship:

_____

____

_____

_____

_____

____

____

_____

_____

_____

_____

_____

_____

...

i have had more chances than i can count

most of which i was too afraid to act upon

in love, in life, in lust—

i have sold out parts of myself

to receive certain outcomes

i have become my own version of a bestseller

for select audiences.

never again, though, will i sell

what i know of love, i know from my before

and the bitter reality of it is this:

i am at a point in my life where every step terrifies me

i am emotionally and physically depleted

from suffering the unknown

i am ready to work any job

as long as it pays me in actual, tangible money

less than a year ago

i left for new zealand to finish my degree

today, i am just another new yorker

traversing the subways home in the early daylight hours

having learned what love really becomes

when you let it live

when you nurture its poetic downfall

like the person you wish you were

all over again, we spin

i am less than

i am only

another artist

in pursuit of desire

a kiss on the forehead goodbye is all you need to take

who can decipher what you need from me

to risk it all for a glint

a glance

Wait, I Think I Might be Sapiosexual.

grand gestures in rom-coms look something like—

2025, i stand on stage

writing in my dreams

with veins as my lines

to guide our betrayals

i do not know how to admit this:

feelings grow like weeds

in a community garden

unmanicured

fertile.

unfortunate in their desperate desire

when i saw anyone

neither of us were where we were supposed to be

you said you were like eyes

i saw you looking when i took my shirt off

the origin of a love-life

i catch myself acting in a way

i can't stop thinking about

what am i to do

without a kiss for sleeping beauty

clearly, there has to be more

it can't just be—

another imaginary fixation

how do i show love

prove love

be love

if you could at least answer me this—

till when will i await

Part Two

NOT A
SURVIVAL
MECHANISM

to whom it may find,

these contents include, for all necessary precautions, the
proper steps to construct an individual body. it is important
to listen closely if you are to survive. these contents
are acknowledgements for the blankets of systems into
humanity—the unpalatable pale glitter on the surface of
windows—and if only it would be easy to admonish homage
in the accomplice of citizenship

i sit and acknowledge

which a self does not mean one— to laminate their
exterior— preventing future visitors from committing
past wrongdoings— as each bone is petition for outward
expansion and to strive in body of capitalist croissants —
(chocolate please)— to briefly conclude and snap and
upload and like and decide who to perceive

i sit and lose knowledge

every letter i scribble is one less i learn, for the despicable,
little notes and lists i leave as president

[head over heal/souls are raindrops sinking from condensed
condensation above my heart, wishing to water another/
righteous contender you yourself is not fair

i sit with open brackets [

— in the craters of the dark side of the moon nuzzling into
the idea of wicked— to worship the warm in stranger stare—
i give to you my fortune for nothing yet perspective of
who dies and lives, stack the insides with throw pillows and
expensive vacations to harmonize in the wonder of empty
homes]
done deal. and this body. sealed and sent

instructions on how to read like a brain tumor
—inhale everything, exhale nothing.

the contents of brain tumors does not make sense.
welcome to the notebook of a prisoner to pages
alongside unmanicured backyards
with damp dreams
if you go the same direction
eventually the origin will rise
where did our fight
separate our personhood
from the obligations of breath,
lines dress up as metal bars
go on blind dates with their observers
across the country
seek a human among the people
the savior places white table cloths
before digging into their meal with finite velocity
reputations to maintain
with honor and descent
a scenery that once painted the walls of my childhood
        bedroom, i once held up familiarity of distance
then, worlds will outlive us all

the point of abstraction and the art of vagueness

i suppose the point isn't to be unclear, but to leave room for experience of interpretation. the path follows this idea. there are gently and subtle hints of which way to turn and where to plant your feet, but if you begin to think too far ahead, you can easily get lost.

if you believe things are changing in your life, they will begin to change. if you believe you are stuck, you will be stagnant. if you think this book is not finished, it will never be

giggles and shits

dead in time square, i was for— once alive
be euphoric
in awe of my little meander
—pressurized awakening—
from the corners of earth
the center has found me
startled and full of
gratitude

the importance of doing things badly

permanence is a quiet exhale. it lumbers around chopping
trees in the swamp and tossing about mud and sticks. shoot,
did i do it again?

personify some unalive abstract force that somehow
intermingles with my bespoke facts of existence.

today, permanence shook my hand in the mirror. wrestled
with the bad-ass nomination. i have 7 words inked onto
my left pectoral, nestled right below the collar bone. over
a mediport scar, which once housed a plastic iv port for the
chemotherapy to fall into me.

a waxing crescent moon hovers. it is the very same leo-rising
moon that shone the day i was brought to breath. followed
by 7 words in my mothers handwriting in three separate line
breaks.

"my heart
is the moon
you planted"

i would do everything i could to protect myself from
subtle disgrace, dishonestly, disappointment, disorder,
disillusionment, and other related "dis" or "un" words.

years later, i awoke two days past christmas, in a rural south
carolina lake house, with another sin on my chest. even more
it was a sin, i decided on, and i graciously desired.

the new day once again reminded me on how being alive
comes with its frequent twists, turns, leaps, and bounds.
this is an unmovable principle of totality that is forever and
unalterable.

drugs and alcohol

at my funeral, i want the there to be a poetry reading about
suicidal ideation. then, all the lines would go straight across
again. horizontal and stable,

what if every letter was a brush stroke of the sky.
every painting was a mountain or valley
tonight i walked home
in the feat of my own size
a proportion against an alley wall—
graffiti written with curse
which is thy very
little mind-like muses
and every story was a fandom of my i

loser

i do not know how to tell you this.
we met as the nation fell

did i tell you i am obsessed
with candles now
it is the wax that burns
not the wick

i do, think you are
a spectacle
settled into my collapsed heart,
disboxed language

i just need to clear my head
the world is ending every day
for dreamers
and suspicious conspiracists

jump

this is my breaking point. my tipping off. i tried, i did. i failed.
i lived.

it could never be the creator
i am the creator
i have always been the creator\
dining behind the cornea
that's it everything is really working out for me
in the best of ways of possible
telling me every direction to go
at the same time
living to break town
in torrential
and outlandish acts
of deep dark incredibly prolific
brutal
don't open palms

whether you laugh at me

or with me i am just here to deflect the barrage of bullets
which hit the insides of eyelids

in the darkest moments of my life, my mother gave me a
notebook that became my way of living within the terminal,
fighting against the oppressor, and rising with vulnerable
resilience.

this is a path we will tread together, the only path you will find.

forget about it all
every damn tiny weeny detail

i can be a white-male anti-capitalist
without writing the perfect capitalist book
with all the specifics and sensory details

this is the truth of my experience for you to take or leave

dickless

i am collecting dics
to put up on my wall
stare at in praise
sharing dic pics
Without any emotion

if i was my name
would be dicless
because a dicless world
is a better world
without any life

i joined tinder again
for the validation again
i got over a 100 likes again
in a few hours again
i will delete it again
what will it take
for a man to want me
not want me

a suicide note from the proofreading department

love is an ongoing, living, draft
we edit, refine, expand, despise
love has never been so exhausted
in their daily routine of meetings
and work and meaningless writings
parenthetical dialogues between
language and words, directionless syntax
love keeps me paranoid, annoyed
in rejection, although there lives
every beat of the soul taking its turn
in the spotlight of gracious, luscious, luminescence
a carousel of dignity
courteous in every detail
vague in careful misunderstandings
i told you, i break easily
love is a tease of falsity
so please leave me with them as a dictator
rage and love got married on Valentines day
because attraction has a little chaos
if it is performed as instructed
i have never done anything like this
with anyone like you
will you be my guide
coaching me every step of the way
as we learn to read
i will comprehend the body as language
eat the syllables

sit at the conference table and wait for the session to begin
i am yours if you want me to be
what you want me to be
i will let the disrespect slide
if you are in it for love,
nothing below
because love is only a human
don't you want to shake their hand

told

i wrote this little story of my life and
it kinda feels like my heart got punched and
got ghosted like, got lightning strike
 i don't even know, i am meant to be so
rather anything to let me go
 pls come on someone give me some tough love
independence— quintessence—contestants
i am never gonna change, imma be a fucking pain uh
uh-iPhone, kill me,

sad rap, that is what my poetry does, it snaps, clap back,
        from all that
dumb shit, hum it, done it, broke it, joke it, uh uh

so fast, so fast, can't stop, wont stop
a mantra, little meditation
on mediocre money, done it for no one
own one, take one, give one, this one
this one—

uh uh i going i'm gone, without dignity, purity, glory,
—what they are gonna call me

notes

for how to tuck in your life
mockup your strife

take the time to revise below:

–the girl

–the guy

–them

–us

–me

price

i am done with ambition
 paying overpriced tuition
i don't rhyme anymore
 with anyone, because it is too easy
do you know the time?

 i forgot to live in the present again
to cherish and not envision
 contrition is a nice word
moving on has never been a strong suite
 of mine

eating chocolate protein in bar and powder form
 to get better
definitions
 understanding my body's lines
criss-crossed undermining hardens

 playing songs from a playlist
i made as time-capsule
 of beatings and dead souls
horse tramples, and snake bites
 those with gratitude can be heroes

this is the first moment I have experienced in 3 years

origin stories of happiness

how has media shifted what we consider to be reality
or "normal life"
the government turning us unhuman
for name's sake
can we at least bake a shitty cake?

is this anything but proof,
 the earth has long since make meal of us
the bees watching their reality tv,
 making honey for us to steal,
the life they will heal,
 is this anything but snoop,
get the sticky ass lore,
 we are dissolved at the core

artificial intelligence has taken my free-will

adult

does it always look like this,
 being grown i mean,
does it always feel this empty /
 pointless.

was my therapist correct when they said I was depressed?

 emails are chiseling me
my heart is an inbox
 should i follow up now
or place you in the trash
 wait who was it in my spam
unsubscribe

 asking for help and people don't respond
please give me a job
 i will get on my knees for you
i just need money
 to feel alive

i am on my way
 to a road on a hill
with dampness and fog

 a place far far away

reaching out, for help up
 onto the stage, free from rage
is this the end of my life
 can this be the end of my life
etched in windows

 begging for security
self-love

 its all about me yeah,
its all about not you, but me
 loove me
lust for me
 live for me
destined to be me
 sippin chamomile tea
perfectly hot,
 going to bed with my sleepy time,

wait no. give me some espresso—
i can not sleep

why

found of wanting
 work and success
not measuring up
 to the bills
and pesty love, pity

 tortured in the most pleasure
gone ghost

 oh withering
wonderful wonderful withering
 with a whiteboard
to erase the writing
 the writing is writhing
withering has written
 living in revolution
revolution, revolution
 valid valid,
power ballad
 tower trembling
own itself
 finding position
in the lenient sky
 the flattened people

god is blessed
 to not be human
keep on chewin'
 soda flavored hi-chew
be an entrepreneur
 live in the sewer
it is all demure

 gluttony is. a. savior's dilemma
the president is killing me.
 everything is disappearing
the world and all its appeal.
 why am i living like this
you do not own me
 or should you think you do

everything that matters

i am done winning awards, the top of everything that matters
 however many glass names
should forever be enough to settle below
 in over my head

did i just say that
 is this getting published
recorded and willingly dispersed
 this could only be the worst thing for you to do
you stupid idiot
 you ill and traumatized
you dead

sold

in a small town where everyone knows everyone, a child with
cancer becomes a bit famous. my return to normal life made
me known for one reason.

a child life specialist at children's hospital, was a constant
presence. whether for ivs, mediport access, checkers games,
or basketball in the teen lounge, _____ was there. she knew
what to say when i felt alone.

terminal

no person can outlive destiny
scrunched noses]
private jet planes
there is an abundance of pollen in the goodbye
to dream in a bed made of bedtime story beginnings
        and endings
uninhabitable of yesterday's achievement
difference in delusions

bags
and what the tumors they carry

forward

the brain tumor is falling in love.
emptiness in its finite glory.

words have always served as a physical output of the
intangible interior. i could never run from anything or
anyone so much as i have learned to run from myself,
digging deeper into despair and displacement. i have studied
rigorously the systems by which we are all entrapped in and
have yet to find any true conceptions of value that do not
yield in "the way of progress". my destiny is choiceless, for
i cannot be one without omitting the other. my legs have
forgotten how to walk and my lungs full of strife. in this
vice i seek sanity, fantasy, relief of envy. if you go forward
relentlessly you forget the trail you tread is built by your tears
and trampled by your darkest desires. this is not a language or
a survival. this is the traveler's itinerary.

i have gone so far from home and it has led me here. to this
end which can be summarized in a 5 page document entitled
resume. it beholds 1467 words and still i am nothing but a
who dares to believe one day they could be enlightened with
recognition that it will not come like this, in this mind, in this
pity. my righteousness and ego are too strong to see their
hypocritical weakness. the only forward is death. the only
awaken is poison. the only medication is defeat.

i retreat into the existence i never knew to be. a forager
for fluid fruition and flightless wings. to fall through the
ground remaining upright. with the weight of the world, i
can only do so much except attempt. attempt. attempt. try.
try. to withstand crumble. destitution. contrition. a font of
my own rising. a front of my own exhale. who am i to be
capable of the utmost agony? i breathe in and out grasping
for meditation. to be great, linear, sure of oneself as their
own individual. to follow the leaders of before, the ways of
worship when i do not know what lurks behind their eyes.
i try, why?

to live i try and i try to live, some version of life that may
never belong in these hands, these words, these crevices of
innocence. i plead ignorance with hope for wisdom. i play
apart the fractures in my palm looking for more. more.
more. yet, there is only less to hold on to. in a world without
value the collective is individual. purity is transformation.
restoration is disembodied. where has gone childish wonder,
imagination, and playfulness?

i have completed you but you have not completed me.
rather cracked my shell into a thousand pieces— enough
to when i can see the rain seeping through. i can taste the
earth on my lips. i kiss and pray for love. i kiss and wish it all
away. i kiss and cry and try some more. abysmal is totality.
the groundlessness has arrived and i am entrenched in a
condition by which i can reside before i must first pack up and
leave. pack my bags and get out and move. move. move and
move from the avoidance of more changelessness.

the fragility isn't the heart, it is the intestine. the veins. the
skin. the floor, the walls, the normality, the mundanity.
the fragility is one and only. one and all.

was

once upon a time i was
a brain tumor
who beheld the greatest
gift of all—
an imagination:
with it carried the power
of the gentle touch
on the strongest wind
the weakness of a thousand soldiers
the pen of a giant little voice

sweet dreams

brain tumors are distinct in their delicious tragedy, special
boy, we eat up gossip of those suffocated from too much
air in their lives and gape at loss like chilled white wine.
brain tumors are a obsessed with hollywood cinema and
live in mansions on the beach to relax during the week
and destroy on weekends and holidays from 2- 5 am the
streets they belong to in the city of needles skin and beings,
bones of skyscrapers no ligaments, artillery constructed to
commemorate the poison of modern medicine, the blessing
it offers, how to meditate from society in devotions of
devolution, i worship rotating doors, reach for the empty of
graves and the cold of caves where cells can talk to tangible
understandings. i understand. brain tumors are dumb, they
tuck you in at night during youth, waiting for age, the stuffed
animal you carried to city market and the bank, were visible
in dreamscapes doing little tap dance on your heart valves,
pumping, beating. disrupting the breathing the heating,
the beating

rain is insane - published in nifty lit literary magazine

100% a curse and a gift, and what the fuck are you chewing
    on
as it goes   the rain   brain drink
    from sewers   taste of security
        over desire   brain inquire
    the rejection
        is my   blood
    sweet   like   red wine   every
    morning   the mind's alarm
    awakens   shakes jumps breaks my legs
    before eyes   open   the truth
    it seeps
into uncharted   darkness   in sunbeam
    embrace
awakened
death
brain pull away   for
brain never did deserve   love
    this is what
death does to the living
    linearity   is fandom   fantoms in
nightmare   brain thought
were dreams   starvation   is cancer's cure
    it kills to live   in comparison
the clarity   of innocence   has left
    tripped. bodies

like skipping stones   with rocks   it sinks
    before the great beyond   arrives
edit   yourself until   you are just
    s.   p.   ace
learn to love the emptiness
    the world is your oyster   slurp
it up and say please and thank you   but
    only adults like oysters   correct
                    you are to
    live in the downpour
              you will regret your ambition
    because rejection is   lifelong
    and
your posture dear boy   and tonight
    is only the beginning of your life
    as the person you ought to be   practical —
    your degree is meaningful   it will give
    you the job you hate   sir.
don't be sad   it is normal to live like them
    in those   squares
with sun tan lotion smeared on their teeth
    keep going   believe in you
and brain thought brain could
    but they got here first   and now brain am
    socially anxious
it not cool   to be proud
    wrinkled fingertips   line these words
someone asked me about my interest.   in 750
    words or less.   except

they don't really want to hear about me, but about how brain
    am them, and anything that is not them is a fault
of my own making   an imaginary world of lost toys
    thief
you are a criminal of desire   you are a criminal using fire
    you are a wire   in my head
forcing dialogue brain never wanted to say
    brain tried to stay   true
it   is   too
    late   with   too
    much
    pressure   pressure   pressure
    pressure   forming coal from diamond
try harder   be greater
    do less   live more   die content
        love is contrite
    the sight of absence   follows footsteps
professional biographies and resumes and gpas. gaps:
land, land, land where are you land
    brain need   land
    there is sand underneath my eyelids
    brain can't   see
freedom on the ocean's current
    a stupid torrent   brain am
only human   beg for mercy   only humans believe
    in courtesy   only humans lie to themselves
    circles and angles
    indigenous knowledge   capitalism
astray and a stranger   fray
    stay   leave

it will pass anyways
     the hopelessness   you petty pretty boy
  listen to the ground
     as the rain falls
     melts into my skin   company
     regretful solitude   ignorant betrayals
     flutter
     like skipping
     rocks   mismatched tolls
     where did all of my socks disappear to?
     their beloved holes and strings   stretch marks
     warms sparks
     brain promise brain am only terrified of life
     not opportunity
     we are all waiting for
     eventual   to embrace
     incessant   is nature   disassociate is
     normal   the mundane
caresses corruption with its tongue   resorting back
     to the known
carries its own price
     vice, vice, vice, vice, vice
                never think twice
                on you will be left
     behind

what

being taken care of / a task of terrible solitude / honey can
you call a consultant? the sickness has arrived in a package
with my name on a black and white wristband thrown on
disrespectfully so the sticky side pulls out my hair - turning
around to go back to the hotel where body can jump between
sheeted kingdoms imagining body am fruitful again /
flying not driving over twists and speed bumps in absence
of friction to the stomachs ache to not be here nor there.
somebody stole my catalytic convertor / the death fumes
taste like espresso body sip obediently.

hey

body build skyscrapers with words
with strings of blankets and piles of pillows
held up by picture frames and forgotten swords
the only limitation is imaginations sorrow
tomorrow body will be in another world
where the milk does not grow so curled
body lay knees to chest, curled

body build realities with thoughts
it is a silly dream driving in these ruts
in attempt to untie the cowardly knots
too desperate to be closed off, unopened
in pristine plastic-- unawaken
to ease the replicating platelet deficiencies

stop

body build sentience with words__medical reign
they reside in my forts
living the realities of my thoughts
there is a soft hurt to healing

i

such a wimpy worship
take another trip to the tantrums
escape into fallen fandoms
body think there might have been a solemn misstep
outside of the safety of my fortress
fluffy, impenetrable, residuals
miserable happiness
long gone paparazzi

it is swell to live by the nonsense
of hopeless romantics and casual semantics
please let me paint your white picket fence
every generation obsesses over the minuscule granules
     of advice
the previous offer—
with each sacrificing the bend
in new harbors and new loves to no end
as every morning body refuse to eat
to let the meat on my bones dwindle
all body ask is for there to be no more swindle
elapse into the twinkle

who

body have flat feet
because there is a weight to the modern mind
in this manufactured time eaten till the shine
body sinks to the ground
to grapple for the surface area
to exuberate friction in the wealthiest way
body am a passenger princess
with my hand hanging free from gravity
to which physics don't apply
when you are already living in submission
of every intoxicating infiltration
body drink tap water
piecing together the lost

when body grow up
body want to be read to
the "happily ever after" because once upon a time
body never wanted to grow up,
when body grow up
body want to be fed to
the indecencies that make up the modern man
fun to play with but not to eat
a manufactured mind / malicious memory
when body grow up
body want to be grown up not sewn up

huh

body have gone and gotten lost in the gander of what it
means to "mean something", without realizing the expense
of hoping to mean something is losing meaning of everything
in its entirety. a body should not need try to "mean
something" more rather by encouraging one's inner voice,
a body may find its voice. it is very easy for the body and
the voice to become separate through environmental and
internal factors that may well lead to permanent dislocation.
yet, the inner voice unites those divorced parts into a singular
spirit. a spirit that has the breadth and depth to permeate
consciousness
for the stranger.

furthermore, the subsequence of great expectations is the
limiting definition of what is and what is not, what could be
and what ought not to. it is a small bridge to make between
"meaning something" and great expectations where many
sized boats may be harbored. one must decide to follow their
inner voice first and can only achieve great expectations
through this method. however, many empty pots of gold lie
when an individual first strives for great expectations
in superior to their inner voice.

this

body must careful and aggressive in all the wrong ways
don't be nice, then you won't be mysterious
show a lack of attention, don't care so much about them and
they will learn to love you the way you are, cause the way
you are is too soft, too gentle, don't settle don't think without
your penis, cause that never works in the way the world
should work

body am sorry body broke your heart. body know this is
only what people say but it truly was me, not you. body was
not ready, and body sensed there was something more body
needed to explore before it became more serious between
us. so, body did what body know how to do best; broke it off
before body got too attached. it is easier that way. moving on
before they even had the opportunity to be close to you.

eventual

body know you. success is her name. it sounds so potent
doesn't it. body am a heartbreak kid who is weak to believe
in himself a little. who am body to demand such unachievable
beauty / or maybe this is her, wait she looks like every other
girl, actually this is turning very patriarchal, let me restart.
body know you. success is her name. it doesn't really make
sense does it. body am a withering wanderer whisked with
wisteria. wow! body know you. success is not for me body
don't believe, at least not that type of success where body
lose myself in the process, of course body have to find myself
first. body don't know you who am body kidding, myself, no,
cant be. body know you. something is her name. body know
body want to be something. someone. somehow. someday.
wow! some of me is in love with what body think too much
about, and some of me is still out there somewhere, probably
online dating, or something like that. body know that this is
different in some way, than what body normally write. body
know that body doesn't follow no rules that tell me what is
the same and what is not the same. see what body did there
cause body don't know you. body know you may or may not
read this, so body wrote it only for you.

compounded is his name. rounded my decimals and painted
my room teel. founded this and that, but still not you.
going is his name. going places, undoing phases, body gave
away because it was the only thing he knew. it had wooden
paddles and it was painted a deep shade of green. body don't

love him, body only wanted him to love me. not anymore, not after what happened when body was born / torn / adjourned. this is too corny, body don't like popcorn because the kernels get stuck in my teeth, and then body can't focus on the movie that my body am supposed to watch. he orders a large with extra butter.

my

body order a new notebook.

less is more and more is less; body confess body am very bad
at tests which of course rests on my ability to eat myself alive
with second guesses, and yes the cancer, that dances around
me like a ballerina on tippy toes, body can't touch because
my own growth was stunted, it spins and turns over and over
with new faces every times unrecognizable to the human eye
that has been grown into by the tumors, so many rumors they
say as they leap and leap again to new bodies with new tights
lined up outside

dirt

body tried all natural orange flavored honey today at the
farmers market and body learned the bees feed the trees and
the trees feed the bees, the gusts feed the bent over trees and
the bent over trees feed the shade that is known for being
directionally challenged, the gust carries the particles into my
eye and the twitching of eyelashes touches the part of me that
finds pleasure in pain. "hey neighbor! what do you feed?"
other than my ears with that sinful music you have been
playing all night long, what do you feed in the campsite next
to mine, stacked like pancakes on a diner plate at 11:00 am,
but body got out, or do you take, are you a taker like the rest
of the mammals here in this national forrest woods and dead
grass and corn
"do you feed the bees and the trees?"

body can tell you what body feed if you are curious: body
feed my hunger because that is what keeps me
happy enough
body feed consumerism and the medicine man who gives me
what body need to be
happy enough
body feed the dirt under my nails that used to be pretty and
body feed the scabs body pick for fun and games, body feed
my ego because body deserve it more than you, body feed the
fear because it is better to live in fear than to not live at all,
body feed interrogation and the wiggling of the bugs body

always squash between my fingertips, body feed the residue
of humanhood, body feed the rocks so body can

medicine

and the cherry on top
"i don't like cherries"
but who gives anything about the individual
and hypothetically if i did like cherries
the cherry on top would be
a
bomb.

on_line

spilling my guts in an online document
"what brings you in today?"

faith
is falling from the sky
but the i miss when
rain was hopeless
and ground fell through
to mars
and building remote control
brains
that will
take over the planet

already taken over the planet
the news is happy enough
so i have faith the future is bright
with wildfire
and i like inhaling pollutants
so i don't mind too much
about the air quality

because peace is about your mindset when
you cannot alter your positionality
and how could i miss the water
when there was no regulation
of windex

observational

sully and mike are the perfect top and bottom couple. their
couple's name would be sike because nobody is supposed
to know all monsters are gay. two monsters who raise a
child on their own, in a world that believes fear is the only
peace sounds a bit too on the nose. tongue and cheek i mean.
by all logic therefore coming out of the closet is just some
joke made by those with no fashion sense. hardened by the
seasoned ice from well drinks and coronas with a slice of
lime hooked on the side. even still the straightest man i know
taught me how to shave my legs and cut my eyelids all the
same. at least monsters have the audacity to give true evil a
run for its money by doing what they do best— terrifying
the bystander with their hot pink stuck on nails stroking their
chin and hips rounded with the little latin american sway, and
the black jock strap that tastes of regret and freedom. at least
evil can after all be glamorous too as does sully with his pink
polka dots and mike with his big eye. at least if you are the
monster you are also the fear and when the search parties go
out for the life i am trying to live, the energy factories shut
down because they have run out of hypocrisy. i will still be
here wearing jeans and a floral button up in my closet.
i will still be rewatching monsters in search of a door to fall
under. a spell to recite. a love to mispronounce. i will still be
watching.

then

the brain sees photographs of those brain grew up, in their cap n gowns, cords draped down the side. a smile plastered plastically on their face as if their brain was just walking by another target mannequin in the office supplies department. the brain sees them, and they look great. as if they are truly prepared to be the adult they were grown to be. their glory makes me only wish to further vanquish in the shadows and to revolt against all.

the media is incessant in informing me how the brain is confirming the contrary. honestly the brain is bewildered at how everyone seems to be walking in all different directions.

brain regret to inform you, brain will not be walking across my graduation stage, at least not now. not when there is so much to see and do outside of the hallmarks of tradition. the brain does apologize for the disappointment brain has inflicted. the brain is walking out of everything the brain has learned. the brain is abandoning the thoughtful.

tradition is marked by our repetitions, an attempt to remember our rewards for existing as long as we have. the brain sees photos of the correct path and brain cripples in indecency. brain tread on the unknown, the palace of uncertainty to find my only exhale-able.

those days, you and i, we were friends only so we could serve
as each other's point of comparison. and more than anything
brain wish for you everything and all of your deepest desires.
brain betrothed myself to the language of dead people.
to the strife of deceit. the treads of tears.

geometrics

it would be lovely to not only see a mirror. even walking
alone, brain can't help but imagine the other half that could
never be reflected by my shadow. how would the light dance
and stumble and change? merge if you will.

the brain has been a man since my entrance to this life
unchosen. and yet, now that brain is truly a man, brain still
acts as a boy when it may prove most. in most steps brain
blunders, falling a few times before getting up and moving
onward. it seems brain greatly enjoys making little wars for
myself when there ought to be no reason to bleed.

the people say brain is a success - the "chosen one" - but the
truth could not be far from alive. brain would much prefer
the term "beheaded" for then there would be no cutthroat
expectations to maintain and uphold. if honor was not such a
pest, it would not be so unbearable to be an individual today.

dreadfully, brain has dedicated the previous years of my life
to accomplishing dreams brain was conditioned and cursed
with. brain have dedicated nearly every waking and sleepless
moment to the concern of rejection or acceptance, prestige or
failure, content or misery. to none of which has sided in my
favor at the fault of my very own hope and self-confidence.
now, without a ground, there is nothing to blunder upon,
but a cliff to hold myself on by the edges of my bloody fingertips.

brain believes this man, if they could be considered a man
at all, is crazy in my head. he obligates me to be responsible
for all of these things to which brain have no real control.
it could be perceived that brain is a hopeless romantic,
incapable of finding another to relinquish in, but the anguish
has far to unravel. brain seems unable to find myself to build
upon without the stabilizers of external praise. the mundanity
is the most devastating heartbreak.

the night before, brain ventured to see the miracle brain and
heard about worms from the sun. little disgusting creatures
really, but at least they are strong enough to provide their
light in times of darkness and uncertainty. brain suppose it
does not matter if one's brain is disgusting if they can be their
own life.

perhaps, brain is the crazy man inside, who is just insane
enough to believe that the crazy man does not belong to me.
perhaps the dawn and dusk could be completed with merry
and love instead of death and doom. perhaps the sunbeam
is only manageable at night and dreams are anchored in the
unobtainable.

occasionally life may force you to try something you never
otherwise would have the courage to pursue. in a place of
utter groundlessness and hopelessness that is inescapable and
somehow also liberatory; it is these times that do make or do
not make the brain of a man or woman as it tests whether one
can find the walls in a desert of obscurity. my greatest fault is
the reluctance to embrace humility as the future.

even more than the stupendous misery of it all, is the why? who shall brain be if "success" does not rush in at once to greet me and paint my portrait? this may be one of the many, since the beginning of time, fundamental truths that define an artist's life like mine. countless of the famous have written about the mysterious, masterful, and wonderful art of rejection on the pathway toward greatness. it is this greatness, that haunts, stalks, peers into my dreams, by which brain am not able to separate myself as shadow. it is this greatness, brain does not understand, why brain is so annoyingly attracted to. brain does believe small lives can too be equally great as large ones.

brain knows it is the very admiration and jealousy of greatness that hinders the creation of it in its origin. the very same reason brain could not begin writing this until the world very well shut its door on me, or the me brain had envisioned.

who cares extravagantly about those who perceive me and the terms by which they are to perceive me when brain has no influence? who am brain to care so consciously about what the image of failure would do to my hideous reputation when failure is a matter of breath? when failure is messily and falsely disguised by the edited and contorted images of each others' bodies. who am brain to postpone love for life despite it being an alternative life to the one brain had envisioned? who am brain to be— that is the very beauty.

brain wishes to be beheaded, by what brain does not know, but it sure sounds grandiose. much more grandiose that of a fellowship or award or honor. and as beheaded, brain proclaims the brain will fail and fall and bleed. as the dearly beheaded every day is the unending beginning.

shall

at birth brain was unforgiven,
  till a brain dressed in the sun.
  far from shudder, liven
  solitude at last was won.
rejection is the ring bearer,
  may them bear witness here.
  love repeats, it's unfair,
  new zealand, a humble sphere.
undead, a dying life pours
  from gutters, drains away.
  gold we ran, encircled dreary stars,
  from saturday farmers' markets' sway.
thy brittle shiver designs honey,
  and butternut filled squash—solemn.
  sequences, residual dewdrops,
  it takes the world to call them.
we may retreat to new edinburgh,
  ironic endeavors of breaking scone.
  if mercy could love me now,
  in solitude, away from each human tone.
in grace, with arrival of nascent light,
  thou patient for the day to rise.
  some hope can become their brain,
  where mildews are brave in what they recite.
a villain made my desires home,
  so venture your brain to pies and cheese rolls.
  might ridicule escape, exhale pacific,
  salt breath and dying leaves, napping prince's tolls.

untouch me, mindless criminal,
  this lore showcases when rain,
  unsolicited skin, tame another,
    crisp pinot noir when dreams came slain.
the ones not remembered are the only
  told stories which remain disdained—
  the quest brain must take to birth,
  and back again, forage along the way.
a leather bound notebook for passage,
  gone, a hidden curse, enchanted lust.
  the law is written in verse,
  unrhymed fall for, make a fuss.
depart today, the underworld,
  awaits your fate, do watch
  your step on headless wanders,
  like love in seconds after—
encounter her while drowning breath,
  their impale before. your spear is flat
  from traveler's dilemmas: where to stay,
  in who to cherish, what to desire, spoken out loud.
entrap me, dear flawed island,
  enact infatuation and understand
  resolution from ego's plan.
my condolences, failure, allure is promise

  demise, surprise me for this journey.
  inside us is integral
  to truth, unsorted realities.

yawn

the first line is not nearly as important as the last. to begin is a
yearn for promise with something or in someone. an ending
has no purpose without its humble origin.

brain arrived in dunedin on february 17th. on that day, my
brain was overjoyed by the possibilities. it seemed the world
was at my very feet simply waiting for me to take the first
step. it was not long before the bliss of expectation between
another devoured my soul.

their name was all of the dreams the brain has had before.
the ending of and brain together, led me to see the untapped
wonder of dreams the brain may not always remember.

brain loved, but my love persisted for the wrong reasons.
it was for security and greatness. too easily, brain forgot
about the cherish of crumble that life endures. no longer did
brian find love for the things that kept my breath in death
times before. the blood brain bled went dry, and the sunset's
brain once fell into a vice.

until one day, in a dreary dunedin brain was sitting below
the one and great, robert burns. writing as a brain tries to
produce anything profound. it was a delusion. suddenly the
brain heard a word though no brain was near. the brain set
my pen to paper and felt a raindrop on my upper lip.
land it did, stop, and roll down my face. a taste of nothing. my
gaze went to the sky where there is a turbulent mind twisting

"where did the joy go this day?" brain says. rain stung my eyes. "why here, why now, am my brain so lost?" only endless at my feet.

right then, the brain swore, and the brain heard a voice say something certain. it must have been some brain near, for it could never have been from my weary and worthless tongue. eyelids sweep like wiper blades and the brain cries. my once pristine leather notebook is now ruined. the words bled into each other as if they never existed at all.

dear god brain do not believe in,"who may i? is this my end?".

awake. orange and lemon soda on my lips. it should not be them leaning above me, lips pursed, eyes closed, then open, and we meet gently. their eyes looked beheaded, filled with a history the brain could never know.

"brain came to say goodbye".
"goodbye" brain whispers.
the hospital door closed. three hours later my brain was discharged. at last the brain could return home from the walk the brain had started nearly 48 hours before.

the brain opens the red painted door to my poorly insulated flat on the leith river. it was humble but it was the place the brain had left home for and that made it mine. already my brain has found me again. the brain crawled into the twin size bed. half of the covers were crumpled and twisted from the previous night's sleeplessness. it was the only home for an insomniac, constant unrest and disease. without taking my shoes off, my eyelids began to fall.

how

breathing is a business. go on, be gregarious. poetry is a
business where you get picked up or picked over. unless you
are a unicorn, to be a poet is to be a businessperson, but if
you are a businessperson, you corrupt your being as a poet.
don't you know it? how do these things work here? to write
the good not real. to feel something else is overrated and
mostly hated and a business betrayal, breach of the contract.
what about monetary compensation? how are you going to
make money as a "poet"? to be a best-selling poet is only
500 copies. how much does that pay? -- a poet has no plot,
no character, no setting, no climax. poetry is small-scale and
disorganized. being a poet is having a terminal illness for an
elderly mind. poetry is a righteous gig not about the riches.
being a poet is an inchworm, creeping millimeters at a time,
until some board (doesn't matter which kind) snatches it up
and crunches it in its beak and swallows the bits and pieces.
poetry is digesting the disgusting and the done to death.
poetry is a proper financial investment for the future because
income is the only life.

smart

it must have been a joke that the brain was special at all.
if my brain could stop myself from joining that awful 7th
grade gifted and talented class. brain should have forced
myself to accept normality earlier, so there would not be such
disappointment as an adult. if brain could go back to writing
journal entries instead of sonnets. brain would be so willing
to destroy everything brain built in myself.

sometimes brain makes pancakes to heal the scars of the past.
sometimes brain drinks. sometimes brain writes, when brain
can. sometimes brain cries and the whole world comes down
on me. some say a man who has nothing owns everything.
some say a man is not a man without a stable job and thick
hands. some say brain is not a man. that is why brain came to
these island green hills. at home brain was landlocked. brain
needed to finally find out the name of my shadow.

the following morning brain sat alongside the leith river; a
moment brain had not taken since brain had arrived here in
dunedin. now leaves paint the ground in a wonderful, almost
childlike palette of crayon like color. the trickle of the ripples
infiltrates my thoughts. brain follows them linearly. let them
go. rest in the noise. the wind seems to have something
against me, because it is always fighting, punching my skin.
it might not even be 8 am. brain sip espresso and rejoice in its
bitter richness.

"oh what a bliss this awakening is!"

quite then brain felt something brain had forgotten. happiness. brain scrambled to open my damp notebook to capture the remnants:

 the stars shone again above my head and for once brain could point to one and pronounce:

"when brain grows up, brain will go there!"

without the little ridicule that functions as a predator to hope.

mri scan

a great lake of white paint
nestled up in the brains lolling hills
where the hobbits drank espresso by the liter
each inch that rose left a residue on the receding roots
each inch that fell gave way to the sprouted

where the little societies
wept into   a stream,
   delta   permeating   each   vein
each bone marrow
whi te st reaks wh ere blo od
gre ets m etal   with em bra ce

squeezed   my childhood stuffed bear
as an illne   ss squeezed a childhood out of me

a team of   medicalese
spit sanitiz   er
poked ugly   cures
with dull ne   edles and sharp liquids
stitched the   etchings of a gravestone
to the cra   nium
dragged   the stone around hospital corridors
sucked pi   ckles and ate gatorade
until i be   came white vinegar in a jar
left for   examination
carried   to the edge of the nightstand

where i   kept each day of the week
in its cute.   lavender container
which swall owed more than it could chew
by the very thing   that made me human

anyways

an elegy to the brain tumor,
upon the other side of love's respite, once bloodlines grew,
        we followed as another.
beyond the dream, we leapt, a drug of love, i won't be there
        when next you call for me.
we live forever   now in evacuation,
 all that i claim   of   any future pride
has gone, has   left   this body, now a shell,
 for whom they cling to closely, nearer still.
a birth discarded, circus in its turn,
 you made   a child what only grief could claim.
in terms   and of conditions, clear am i
 of what   i must achieve through chronic strife.
alas, your   sword still pierces through my tongue,
 like twins in birth, the   same inheritance.
an urge to fall, left   proud upon the cliff—
 become you more?   for   shame, i still adore
the blur of what we   were,   impossible,
        so-called forbidden   destitution's end for may
declare, no   longer apart of us / this could go on for
        eternity

123

a commuter train bound forever: back and forth -
   published in 12th street literary magazine

$2.90
a man yelled after i have a heart
i am good i need sesame chicken
which seems reasonable cause for
Scraps and to contend such impur
ity lips open to respond with no n
oise to retort could barely muster
Swallow two cheese slices, new y
ork style bent in half the silence f
olds your cheeks traded for faint
cherry medicine licking envelopes
Signed my love

$2.90
a man i belong to called
repeated the same abbre
viations and exclamation
s! of young ignorance th
at could be rescinded back
these are the delusions of
ego we where the depend
ent vanilla syrup compuls
ion of heavy pieces of furn
iture from house to past ad
d fresh paint and hardwood
floors and a pool memory a

dwindle like dining room ta
ble candles unlit conversati
on unknown truth

$2.90
less of the man in citations
of a body (mla style) use ea
sybib.com to lighten the fo
rmat to recount rusted pen
nies dipped in ketchup to r
esolve them as new and shiny
picked up off eyeballs tails si
de up leaves on the pine stat
ue are picked by nature to ch
ange and flutter die under a s
oulless crunch who satisfies t
he soul into something great
er than abolition absolutely a
nything they indeed still have
a blunder to see out deconstru
ct the spine of the cyclical how
to notice people

$2.90
three autumns chronology:
begin to sink what the sub
lime could tell fortune alo
ne in impulsions natures s
entience hereby renounce
what you thought love cou
ld do for the exclusionary

$2.90
a french couple asks direct
ions to the statue of liberty
i do not know here the bro
wn green lady who braves t
he shores fiction i bid them
a swell day only what is unsp
oken to who cannot write i
miss i am no politician follo
wed. analyzed. recorded. i he
ard not this idea to pay for li
beration, nick at nick's barb
ershop referred to me as my
boy he snipped and clipped
the dead skin i drew my sch
edule on a poster when told
to represent knowledge quit
e prolific, a routine of cuttin
g loose ends a boy younger th
an me in vietnam who had ne
ver touched blonde before like
monthly periodicals or newsle
tters to obliterate what was gr
own in typical fashion these s
ame words my boy uttered by
brain tumors

like

if brain wasn't hopeless there could be none—
romantic as the trees, absent of soil.
blood does boil till fame, obtain.
uptown deviants come. please persuade hallow.
they sink these hills to heaven— perspective.
forgive loyal bitch weakening for crevice.
sand flies under my skin in savage love,
serve dinner at five. let hunger drive each dream.
a casual blunder— deform linearity,
if brain should walk in a straight line— onward,
my feet would turn around and weep away.
another religion who does dumb regret reform.
unfair poignant purpose, an albatross,
thy curious in flutter, serenade the failure,
usual detriments for happiness— cloudy pill,
thy feet would carry me there, underwater— homo.
reside in cure, impure at heart, to forgive oneself,
in rejection, in discretion, between villages.
if brain could talk to sheep brain would ask why
the ground is full of dirt and a sky of glass.
one day, i'll go on a ship with eyes dry,
the crew might hang a mindless soul to mass
unlike sorrow we follow empty piles of—
alone the traveler's hurt whispers, linger,
to wish for anguish, a rich man's desire:
fortify every, expel any
one who speaks agony may retire to himself.

what relinquish do you marry rubble?
brain imagine land so barren, before colony,
a person is self-less without a place to be.
thou wear a suit on frigid beaches, bright day,
be late to roam for laminated skin freaks.
be great, not lame, in dead, dirty silly aliens.
relief you haunt distant sound of waves— bye
enough abandon freedom, they will be okay
with headless hearts and weary veins tonight
'twas their belonging sacrificed ago
to which in-value measures next to any,
then turbulence and brain became close friends.
a job that pays for skeletons to walk by
a year of life let pass by on its own.
is there a point on this tiny sphere?
to climb without being impaled for homage
rereading summaries in change— so long
my honey, farewell drizzle. follow my scent if
belief is real, for otherwise brain lost my spoken
exclusive selfish dumb death, brain envy compassion
to clarify we are made of dirt?
and water. born in wood and rock— to fathom
an end is the same to forget beginning
clasp in fear, we shatter solitude
—deserve blank pictures, surprise
brain kept a speights for drink, doomsday attempted murder
that itch will never recede, its pride too large
for rules be law; brain wrote a poem and folded
a paper plane and flew across the world
for nothing to come alone to me, all the way out

brain cried the first exhale brain felt life
the droplets fell from thunderclouds below
courage held hands with sweaty dreams
curiosity how'd you do?
a thorough exam human
please

soft

when things begin to spin
in the big, giant, world of fun
the sunshine machine has arrived
and you have been expecting
to start seeing stars
in the great big city again,

you're on the up
in and out
of the big
bad, and
dangerous

now go and get out of here,
live your big, bad, boisterous of fame
succession and destiny
they are all waiting for you
out there in the big bad globe

part of you thinks plucking
little fragments in this big bad document
to save yourself
from such self
the happiness
comes from seeing those
you love most dear
be so brave

in their own special
little way
full of flowers, and bad ass

it is the ultimate
of one

ok

so
 there
you
go
out
 of
this
 big
bad
 rut
you
 have
been
 in

american lessons' on vietnam

sun nibbles toes and fingers
limbs won't work right
bending outside the ways
motorbikes race down my alcohol filled veins
a public entity meant for utils
domains, spitting and throwing pineapple rinds, the heat
      blisters
brain like combat boots
bruise cement sidewalks they lease, an airplanes seat soaring
      in solitude, back frozen and curtled, from exploitation,
      exploration,
drunken passageways, don't touch
them with love—detestable doormat
desire— blood soaked
passion for the derailed, turned into fruit punch
spiked for living, salty bone broth
own lung and peace formatted into death
currency as, the absence of ice to melt—
 inhales
no longer differentiate the concern of loss
purpose is nomad who speaks the future
a language of soulless—individual
corruption, eviction of the oneself
is enough to devour
:
sweat blossoms a
lotus, a new beginning droplet

side of temples on the sides of skulls
takes time going, falling, releasing
leaving sticky, salty residue
i lick for flavor
arrives unquenched—more
i am dry, shriveled, selfish
sweat carries the toxins with no hands
skin has attracted to itself
vanquish of company
release utopia imprisoned
in personal design
succumb architectural
undermining and suicidal
thoughts on the top of skyscrapers
plead—
dedicate language to its victim hoods
everybody has a partner
love and hate and regret and ignore
:
a writer can only love
aches in their pen,
writhing humble confines of 9
by 11 inches
means less to be ugly,
pointing may begin
sweat soaks paper, stains its contents
blurring spaces into words—
utilized to expel
little pierces of the footsteps
you followed for safety

landed in disruption
who have neglected to let
go of the one you could,
decided to undo—
this is the skeleton,
selection of individual shortcomings
to overheat until
combustion is necessary
for all relevant
proceeding to proceed
fair warnings however
it can be impossible to distinguish
sweat
from tears
it requires careful considerations and surface judgment
vindication and intent manipulations of the "other"
reading, rereading emails
i want gone
the insides of
vice, i need gone
tonight! by morning i beg
i must stop falling—
to defer due to processing time
and transaction fees, defer dreams
the horizon will come and skate your palm
firm and strong, they say "job well done"
and they consume you
tell you destruction
you are undone
unmade and divine

ridicule, unravel,
into forever
it is time for you to go
sweat until your mouth is dry
and don't come back to this house,
of wealth— caution
there is danger in life
you can buy a sim card there
then identity may flourish there
find us here

anesthesia

photo of the inside of your hand, 9 screws— transcription

of   those calloused biologies father, amuse transcription

there was nothing

there was pure

there was less

who   made many

goin'. on dates when fair seems unjust, no use, corruption

won'tyou believe me, i don't dare care, misconstrue

       transcription

there was solace

in   solitude and solemn

there was any

one's taste in the sugar along the glass

there was intoxicated body and each other around the next

       door neighbor

open the door with your bruise will you, far few, left behind

sit   down with loneliness the lover, for you, transcription

there was a bar sipping tap water

there was pass- away and the

scent of language in search

of   breath to be

the   color of dried hope lingers low, undo, transaction

inspiration. is not for the weak, how do, transcription

there are summits

with. recently diverted

the   call of purpose beckons me there, issue, commander

follow   insight for the night is young, tissue, transcription tectonics

to. occupy

attached   to my pinky toes

pointed.   in exchange

cloudiness.   speaks known tongues in whisper, for you,
        destiny

recall.   those tales of forrest scents rise, did you, transcription

there is decision

in   what was from.   what could not be

woof

a
number of us
collected and praised
our cinnamon teeth. assigned
 to outdo each other until we
 wither and perish. to care
about the placement of commas and

improper grammar more than one's identity in themself.
concentration is the finely curated demonstration of
intelligence where perfection is the only home a body can
sleep, yet the public rage r remains unhoused and shaking
from the gust of new york whipping the scarf around my
neck and rag tightening and walking around rockefeller
center until the building merge and blur and are blown rag
away like a dandelion on a summer afternoon. celebrities
shaking hands with lifeless on every street. ra narration in
nosebleeds. feed me carbon and give me the flu. seal each
town entity in zip locks and rage make sure to get all the
air out before you begin to breathe in the fire's fume.
rage rage rage rage rage ra

it   is   christmas   eve   in the empty bank
            accounts. watch the taxes may eat you like moths
            swarm the sun to keep

safe

—it's warm enough.
—for the bones to stop their creaking
—when the bend down
—will body ever be again
—sold in a garage sale
—for 50 cents
—true value always goes forever undelivered
—delinquent morbid
—chasing snowmelt to the sea
—whittling a conscience
—into fixation
—quilted patriarchy
what may you run from
what may you fear
what may you desire
the makers: playing hide and seek
body thought there was a spider in my tent so body swatted
        and punched and kicked until body bled blue gatorade
it turns out
the spider
was in my head
crawling
repelling
biting
buying and selling
sleeping on a wobbly table
in a hotel lobby

applying a world of tragedy
to a single response....
waiting
for the wetness
to be syrup not blood

preservation

cultureall
                exclusive
        appropriation
rearranging old hallucinogens
to stimulate new architecture
tree bark
outlines of decency
neosporin oozing from its wounds
sunken soldiers ask not to be stepped on by lost wanderings
        but instead of pummeled by soul searchers who are too
        used to being gone
skin
on skin
hood up, head down
floating desolate demand- dawn
body have an attachment
to the
disposable
the dispossessed
dandelion bulbs inches
above the waters tumult
tempting fate
wishing to vanish
the bug bites make me feel less than fiction
dried fruit under my tongue
body can't
talk right now

overripe moonshines

body yearn for you miscellaneous stones

that fell from some god

they never

belonged to

strawberry ice cream is the filling of my dug out/

      extracted interior

chewing on mint leaves body found on the side of the street

honking at the harmony between lips

which direction does the inhale permit

sitting on

tombstones of the past names that once enlightened my

      phone screen to mean something

absent from who we are

we are

this rotten from the pressure to grow

be ripe you

be ripe you

body dried

you and shrunk

flavor!

be ripe to linger longer on my tongue

body brush my teeth again because nothing matters the first time

for at least the causality of pain

is ripe with

something

here

it is about to arrive
perforated for easy separation
like the delicate breakage of a kit kat
it is coming
the end of inspiration
milk chocolate covered wafer
too beautiful
too done with
recited and notable and idolized
in the alchemist i omit
utterance whistles when lost
a slow eerie sound
the heart is about production
the former and foreground
forgive the later and background
guilty everything's trying to be anything
except something before
i blister and hum

suave

encased lips
here is your destiny
charming, disordered
astounding little serendipity
never to return
vulnerable

do you know how to distinguish
any small suit
or he
     told
me

to kill a darling

epiphany soup

4 bay leaves
sprigs of rosemary
thyme
brown sugar
a whole butternut squash
one can of corn
pre-cooked bacon pieces
heavy whipping cream to texture
salt and pepper to taste

mix and heat till smooth
have you ever held it?
bloody and ugly
loose and all together in some celestial fortune

pull down, hard and then separate
then painful return

ok pt 2

the only thing greater than imagination is inspiration.
perspiration is the only natural cleanser. surrender is a
dandelion's delusion when a wish is made upon. the title trips
on its own glory.
there is no structure yet. respite is a foe of washing
motionless. countryless and incapable of proper archetypes.

on and on

preferability would be forever,
on and on and on some more,
more it would be more after less
more before it boils over the spaghetti
tossed a noodle at the fridge
if it would stick
preferability will be forever
when i gave up ambition for hot chocolate
left to chill with thickness of syrup
preferability is too sweet
for regular miracles such as consumption
for human regress dressed themselves
as their preferred weather— cloudy day
mindful invisible and altogether alone
preferability should be forever

ars poetica

select all, copy, paste. cutaway at edges until you have left
a reflection of a mere body. this mostly results in more
than what was given. i cling to more than what has been
discovered, found, loved before. the slow sipping of an
unknowing until some sort of recollection can be relapsed.

writing is my remission of illness in all its vast formations.
it is why some travel to the desert to exist in the absolute
empty nothingness. then, they can see themselves and their
purpose more clearly. only when vitality is waiting, can we
look closer at the larger picture.

in other words, "a kiss on the cheek" or even the forehead
for that matter. as long as there is some sort of boundaryless
affection at work that can nor be defined or released
completely. the heat screams with its arrival. the cold is
always nearby awaiting gratitude and fame.

similar to cycles of starvation and binge, my writing pervades
all normalcy in acquaintance of foreign appreciation and
discomfort. nothing will ever be enough, and this is all it can
ever be.

i take on too much and decipher what is left-over from the
shroud of spineless capitalists and inescapable meanings
we must succumb among. to abolish the refinery of simple
machines in exchange for imperfect intangibles.

typical of hybrid forms mixing the textures of poetry,
comedy, and prose to construe the multiple layers of grief.
most often, utilizing radical vulnerability and honesty to
devour the taboo and force awakening between the mind,
body, and society. writing is a hostel.

a collective act, as much as an individual shortcoming and
becoming. in this way, there are no laws, no fictions. the only
limits are the imagination of destiny and reality. my identity
plays as large a role as any in the anchors of each syllable.
inspiring and conspiring them to exist in their own shape.

i construct the undone, the revolution, the redefine of
the very possible. looking to what needs reconciliation,
reinvigoration, and reclamation, my writing is not just words,
but a leap through the betrayals of sanity and artistry.

what i mean is what i do not know and may never find. what
i find is that i do not know what i wish to mean. it is a plural
verse of its own being.

poetry, in its most radical form, is a refusal to be defined by
anyone other than oneself. it is the act of unveiling the truth
hidden deep within us, of amplifying voices that have been
drowned out, and of setting ourselves free.

the soul of rejection is the heart of a bestseller

compliment sandwich

of sorts
filling in the pieces is the method of existence
rifling through paperwork, trying to add detail
can be a dreadful task
when you have been running the senses
to find your own

factory
mull out in cubicle\
proper lines all in order\
going downhill in a flat city\
stamp, press, send, place product on shelf\
for average indulgence, by the average american writer\
caught listening to sinful appreciations and abstract
        realizations\
over tangible income and momentary rectification of human
        actions\
i need it out here

        in all this void

earth_tones
whoever named the colors possessed too much power
for their arbitrary diction
what do i need to prove i am a writer

shiny gold and stolen identity
or rusted metal prone to infection

meditation
drone voices
enter trance
dear savior
why time can be so wasteful

i cannot please everyone,

love is an ongoing, living, draft
we edit, refine, expand, despise
love has never been so exhausted
in their daily routine of meetings
and work and meaningless writings
parenthetical dialogues between
language and words, directionless syntax
love keeps me paranoid, annoyed
in rejection, although there lies
every beat of a soul taking its turn
in the spotlight of gracious, luscious, luminescence
a carousel of dignity
courteous in every detail
vague in careful misunderstandings
i told you, i break easily
love is a tease of falsity
so please leave me with rejection as my dictator

rage and love got married
because attraction has a little chaos
if it is performed as instructed
i have never done anything like this
with anyone like you
will you be my guide
coaching me every step of the way
as we learn to read
i will comprehend the body as language

eat the syllables
sit at the conference table and wait for the session to begin
i am yours if you want me to be
what you want me to be
i will let the disrespect slide
if you are in it for love,
nothing below
because love is only a human
don't you want to shake their hand

A national disaster weary in anguish
regard for hives on hills, highway straights
retired monsters wake in starless evening
bewitch tingle spreads through the economy
ignore me and it will thicken
when destitute is leaving your home, the backdoor slams
supply recoiled in remorse for its pressure
reconciliation in exchange for its measure
low barriers to entry / input costs
Red lights are great for a kiss
rotate these gears and find oil
soaked rigidities
demands— the price of a species
is commodity and price tags,
reckless disadvantage,
and value propositions.

good morning,
i can't wait to tell you
how wonderful of morning

to make something of
if only the cloud people could
stay in bed too
with the deadweight exhale
armed nonetheless a person to fight for

i bet you are confused, not in a sexual way ofc (well, who knows),
i mean confused, as in lost.
just as we all are, all of the time, at all stages of our life.

line breaks don't solve everything
that is what my professor told me
to my right is a 34-year-old flower
their richness of dramatic pauses
completely unexplored,
to my other a 22-year-old promise
we may never speak to contracted gold mines
utilized for digging in the dirt and extraction
split between pathways and neighborhoods
steep to soar
it is bitter to need more

line breaks don't solve the world's problems
to my meditation practice and breath work
still must rise, and get to work today,
at night I bleed the color of kingdoms:
take away the truth
take the minute mutation
extrapolate
metropolitan areas

in the end
be weary of
believing to much of what people say
line breaks don't solve anything

that is what my professor told me.
bc this is serious
 for the sake of journeyless officials
feels like somebody called me baby
 underworlds look more like sky
hey, hey, that is why we must try
 to live on, empty

 spit on roaming in the light
sewing a bedtime story
to spit on the seam
 what may reap
 The oldest stare in America
steer clear and be honest
split fire
and run your route
 burn the way you are born
 what may creep
 the expensive is cheap

rainbows for beginners
-i heard if you climb to the top you will see everything wrong
          with the world
-i heard if you jump off the top it will take you so long to hit
          the ground, the Earth will be consumed by water

-and you might be the only human left
-i didn't believe them, so i am on my way, right now
-i heard i am innocent
learning how to be so selected
the most pretty kind
the least lovely kind

notes from those who have impacted me most:

excerpts from my mother

amidst the darkest hours of the early morning beast a light
sleep, the sound of a ping awakes thee. an enchanting lyric
awaits from thy seed.

the incoming text spun me into a mode of self-reflection,
to an earlier time when a wise friend told me, "a miscarriage
was the body's way of teaching it how to become and be
pregnant." little did i know after that emotionally painful
experience would i end up giving birth to the most perfect
baby boy! i always thought i wanted a girl. a mini-me.
amidst giving birth, i was told it was a boy. at this news,
i remember shouting out, "what am i going to do with a boy?"

we had names picked out for both scenarios. rowan shae mott
if a girl. rowan finn mott is a boy. "finn" won out! and i must
say, being a "boy mom" has proven to be the most rewarding
success story of my life.

upon learning of the second pregnancy, i made a promise to
myself and unborn child that i would take the good from my
parents and dismiss the not so good, seeds of change, break
the cycle so to speak.

my parents were an amazing example of a beautiful
marriage and a relationship of a generational time. it was an
everlasting, undying love story even still after my father's
passing in 2010. my mother's devotion to her husband has
forfeited her mind to that year of losing him. they not only
exuded love, devotion and support for each other, but for all
five of their children.

growing up in this environment, i realized i craved
friendship with my parents. specifically, my mother. do not
misunderstand, she is and was an amazing mom. she is kind
and caring. she never swore, she was involved with pta, bake
sales and church. she was a socialite. she had a network of
lady friends who regularly golfed together and played bridge.
my mother was what i believe to be my biggest supporter! i
love that piece of childhood. as i grew and became more of
my own person, the realization came to me that i could not
tell my mom "anything." same held true with my dad. he was
a provider, a funny man of few words. when he spoke, it was
quality. he didn't often give compliments, so if you received
words of affirmation, it was since my mom, they kissed every
morning before he left for work and when he came home
every evening a drink was ready and waiting for him, dinner
on the table and again they kissed. we needed or wanted for
nothing. dad always made sure we were happy. he played
games and goofed around when we were young and he
helped with homework as we grew older, he offered advice
if asked, he performed chores on the weekends and took the
family out for occasional sunday drives. dad was a gentle man
with devoted, life-long friendships.

remember when i said a generational relationship?

my parents provided us with a chore list to earn an allowance.
if chores didn't get done or if we paid disrespect there were
consequences. consequences might've come in the form of a
spanking. delivery methods depended on the severity of the
bad behavior. i remember tools like, a brass shoe horn, belt,
ping pong paddles, hand on bare bottom. it was pretty rare
that a swat ever happened but understanding it could,
we respect our parents.

now, i digress earlier in my writing.

that promise i made to myself and my unborn child, soon to
be finn.
i vowed to form a friendship with my child. a mother
child bond that would withstand the test of time, a loving
supportive connection based on trust. i wanted my child to
feel comfortable to talk, share stories, ask for help, and have
deep conversations about anything! i also committed to never
striking my child. for the life of me, i don't remember why
i was ever spanked, therefore i never understood the point.
during my pregnancy, i knew the relationship with my child
would be one of mutual respect. respect is earned. it is not
built from fear nor automatic.

once finn was born, i deepened the promise to myself and the
world. i was dedicated to raising a human that was sensitive,
fearless, creative, respectful, kind and independent. through
the miracle of life, growth and circumstances, it worked.

fresh out of what finn refers to as "the never-ending divorce," i was a single mom, learning how to be independent, work full time and take care of a young boy. it was a time to face fears. one of those fears is needles. for my fortieth birthday, i decided to surrender to my fear and stamp myself permanently with a tattoo. a florist at the time, i chose my favorite flower for no other reason but the namesake, the black-eyed susan. finn and i talked about the flower and at the age of five he asked me to place a small heart in the center, so i did.

little did i realize this tattoo would be the symbol of my life to come.

the black-eyed susan is more than just a pretty flower. it is a self-seeding flower, a beauty of its own kind, associated with the warmth of summer and sunshine. it is hardy, resilient, adaptable, versatile, and thrives in a variety of environments from meadows, woodlands, prairies to roadsides. what is also known as the gloriosa daisy, it has medicinal qualities and is a floral symbol of triumph in the horse world. yes, i said horse world. for those of you who know me, my first love and spirit animal is that of a horse.

the petals of my black-eyed susan, hug my universe, my heart, finn.

when finn was diagnosed with brain and spinal cancer at the age of thirteen our world as we knew it shattered to what felt like the depths of earth. grounded and etched in memory forever, along the drive to children's hospital my boy asked me if he was going to die. my response was, "not on my watch!" fear and pain were eminent. the journey of sickness, treatments, and healing seemed to be never ending. my seed, my son, my heart, my center needed the black-eyed susan's strength.

the soil and seeds of my youth taught me what it means to grow and harvest flora of my own. i kept the promises made to myself, finn, and the world. the struggle of our journey is a beautifully written lyric of life. the strength, resilience and adaptation to overcome and triumph is undeniable. the person who has been the center of my universe is my life, soul, fuel, sunshine and my why. the fearless, sensitive, independent, creative seed was planted and grown through life. nurtured with love, water and sunshine.

now....

look how that boy "i didn't know what to do with grew!!!"

thriving at being the creative artistic poet, the successful author, the independent world traveler, the sensitive advocate, and the fearless survivor and activist. if you look beyond what you see there are signs everywhere. i am the black-eyed susan.

excerpts from my father

i love my son. the gentlest and loving of any human i have
encountered thus far, a real gift to humanity. finn's 22 years
of life has been nothing short of remarkable.

we gave it our best i think, but eventually i understood that in
order to be a great dad, i must end an unhappy marriage and
start over again. this was the summer of 2006 and when we
were both tested, a single parent and a four-year-old son.

my career is guiding fly fishing trips, working 7 days a
week for most of a 7-month long busy season starting in
the early spring and continuing through the late fall. it was
challenging to find the time for his care especially during
the summers, with no immediate family here in colorado,
or close neighbors to assist and the demanding hours i was
putting in to pay the bills. during the school months, it was
often a race in the morning to keep us on time, both to class
and to the river. i remember driving through the elementary
school drop off lane while pulling my drift boat behind, and
the disappointing looks i received from the principal as i put
the truck in park and got out to grab finn's bike from inside
my boat. "you cannot stop here!" she would remind me. but
finn and i did the best we could together, and these early
challenges helped shape the incredible man he would soon
become.

finn was asked to do a lot on his own early in his life, cuddler yes, but i was not a coddler, and my parenting style was that if you want it, you might have to do it yourself. that included cooking and meal preparation when he was still very young as i was just not able to always drop my busy schedule and help. i remember finn asking me to crack the eggs in the pan so they would not break to make sunny side ups as i refused. "if you want to learn to not break the eggs, you must practice on your own to get better" i encouraged but also knew it was hard for him to hear. there were many of these moments that were hard on him, but they nurtured his young independence and early maturity.

i would pay for him to be in after school care till 6 pm on my parenting days, and i was often still late to that. they would charge me $1/minute as i was persistently late as my days ran long, often to uncontrollable circumstances with clients showing up late, or bad weather and getting off the river on time. my poor boy is almost always the last one to go, standing by the door waiting....

then we would head home to prepare dinner, complete homework, shower, and so much more as i rushed to clean out my boat often in the dark, then email clients, send pics, rig rods and prepare for my trip the next day. finn learned self-accountability at a very young age, and it was an important skill that would play a much more influential part of the life challenges that lay ahead in his life.

we were in avalanche certification class in the winter of 2016, learning to read snow, use beacons and be safe while ski touring in the backcountry near vail when finn started having his first symptoms of his quickly growing illness. we stayed in the loft of a cabin deep in the white river national forest, accessed from a ladder affixed to the wall, not an easy climb up and worse going down. nevertheless, my son would go up and down multiple times every night as he was already suffering from diabetes insipidus symptoms and an unquenchable thirst.

in the next few weeks, he started to have frequent dizzy spells, balance issues, vision problems and just did not feel right. doctor after doctor mis-diagnosed him with sinus infections, migraines, the onset of puberty, and others. i was determined to find the cause of his ailments, and only after a second visit to the 4th doctor, was an mri ordered. they just were not looking for brain cancer in a 13-year-old boy.

i'll never forget the call from vail valley hospital. "hi pete, how are you? where are you right now? i have some news about your son's mri. we need you to pack a bag, a bag for a maybe a long time as your son has a lot going on in his head. he has two large brain tumors. we have a room ready for you at children's hospital in denver, you do not need to even check in, just head there as soon as you can."

the old cliche of what doesn't kill you, but rather makes you better; the impact of his battle for his life was a powerful force that finn chose to not allow to abate, but rather strengthen him. never negative, angry or bitter, he became grateful for every precious second, and used the immense terror of his diagnosis to empower him. perhaps too some of the extra things that were asked of him in his earlier years now were immensely helpful to allow him cope with such overwhelming circumstances.

since beating cancer, finn has been fueled from his illness to make a difference and repay the support he received when he needed it the most. in our local community, finn was an incredible public speaker, raising money event after event including the roundup river ranch where he attended 3 summers in a row, and benefiting other children also from donations as they faced similar life threatening illnesses. his method was kindness and compassion and he affected so many; many of whom have shared back to me emotionally his impact.

finn has overachieved in every category, all the way back to when he was just entering elementary school and struggling single parents. nearly straight a's, extra circulars, engaged in his community, charitable organizations, volunteering, participating in highly competitive sports and always loving his family. he did it all and although his childhood was not always easy, and he woke up every day always willing to give his all.

even with all his accomplishments, he kept his humility and was in disbelief when he was awarded the highly acclaimed el pomar scholarship attending the competitive and respected academic colorado college the last four years. two service trips to africa teaching english and distributing school materials they cannot afford from his own earned money, a junior ted talk, 3 self-published books, podcasts, and recently a graduate fellowship at the new school in new york city, it's hard to imagine him accomplishing more at his still young age.

i will never forget his first semester abroad in his junior year of college, copenhagen for nearly 6 months, alone in europe where neither of us had been able to afford to visit prior. but as usual, finn accelerated it, requesting to be flown to florence, italy with only a backpack and a filtered water bottle, to then travel to denmark by himself. venice, bern, frankfurt, amsterdam, hamburg, and more, while staying in hostels, organizing his transportation and meals, to finally reach his school weeks later where we mailed his possessions in a cardboard box. simply amazing at 20 years old, a true testament of his sustained courage from his childhood and his illness, he believes that he is truly capable of accomplishing anything he wants.

as i continue to guide fly fishing trips, before we even get to the boat, my clients still ask about finn, so excited to hear all about his latest achievements, and not able to hide a deep exhale that he has continued to stay healthy. i can't agree more, humbled to be his dad. i hope a great dad, and a positive influence of his life's journey one might predict has only just begun.
i love my son; he is nothing short of remarkable.

a poem from my best friend

this tree
has grown and shed
many leaves,

this tree has entered
its last era
as a sapling.

it reaches down and out
breathes up
into a changing sky,

alive,
expanding and decaying
this tree has its own patch
in that big endless forest

—Margaux Stavney

ACKNOWLEDGMENTS

Thank you to the muse of existence, to all of those who have challenged and inspired, those who have held and hurt, those who brave what they do not choose. Thank you to the Earth, the people, and the rain. This book would not exist without the people who reminded me that stories are meant to be lived, not sold. Thank you to my parents, best friends, and support network.

To my mentors, teachers, and fellow writers—thank you for showing me that literature is about truth, not trends. To my friends and chosen family, who have stood beside me through every draft, rejection, and existential crisis—you are the reason I keep writing.

To the poets, comedians, entrepreneurs, rebels, and troublemakers who refuse to let the market define their worth—this book is for you. And to the publishing industry: thanks for the material.

Thank you to Lethe Press for giving me this incredible chance to speak.

FINN MOTT is a queer, cancer survivor who contemplates whether success is worth selling their trauma for a neatly packaged story—then decides to burn the whole system down instead.

Acclaimed poet, entrepreneur, standup comedian, and literary disruptor Finn Mott takes a scalpel to the publishing industry in this sharp, unflinching manifesto. Blending personal reckoning with industry critique, *How Not to Be a Bestseller* is a battle cry for writers who refuse to be commodified.

www.ingramcontent.com/pod-product-compliance
Lightning Source LLC
Chambersburg PA
CBHW020158090426
42734CB00008B/861